Johnson Chronicles
Truth. My Penis. Tall Tales.

Peter J. Harris

INSPIRATION
HOUSE

Copyright 2017 Peter J. Harris
ISBN: 978-0-692-87883-5

Table of Contents

/5/ Foreplay
/9/ Perfect Fit
/17/ In The Morning
/23/ First Go-Round
/29/ Watch My Balls
/35/ When Johnson Gets Blue
/41/ Skin Off My Johnson
/49/ Johnson Time
/53/ In & Out
/57/ Praise Song
/63/ Head
/67/ Vasectomy
/73/ Pops and Them
/79/ Mythical Johnson
/95/ Hair (Wet Dreams)
/101/ Truth and Tall Tales
/113/ Up for the Down Stroke

Johnson Chronicles

Foreplay

Autobiography is Briar Patch, catalyst, and sometimes terror-tory for the following vignettes, intellectual dozens, vows, and affirmations. But autobiography don't mean the truth, the whole truth, and nothing but the truth, so help me y'all! Confessions veer off into wanna-be hindsight. Memories flower into archetypes swapping gossip. Serious up in here. Silly. One minute ranting. Next second, nodding my head with a knowing insight. Ain't nobody interested in my joint.

Confident enough, finally, to go ahead and solo as my way of sorting through the cacophony aimed at our penis, our Thang, until emerges the voice familiar as a trusted big brother, slinging enough wisdom that we can hear a common sense that inspires us to hum along.

My vantage points, my perspectives, flow from the mind of a straight man with a vivid imagination, healthy fantasy life, and rich erotic experiences. If I've gotten it right in any way, the Johnson Chronicles resonate for a wide range of dudes, with orientations and predilections different from mine. We all have been searching for elemental, whole maleness. We've all mistakenly let Johnson be our guide – following our little head instead of our big head, as some of my Sacred HNICs would say. We all have risked taking solos that convert or nurture the cacophony.

Red-bone to blue-black. A man with a small penis. A brother with a Johnson big enough for a double take. Dudes always hollering What up Dog! Or fond of saying 'my nigger' this, 'my nigger' that. Mid-level elders, rolling HNIC or African American off their tongues like the Baby Boomers they are. OGs in their 60's and older, straddling Afrikan, Brother, Negro, and Colored, as they embody the evolution of society from Jim Crow through Back-to-Africa, Civil Rights, Black Power. Ambassadors from all generations, who claim the Life Movements that turned some of us into vegetarians, Eco Witnesses, urban farmers, and radicals who vibed through ideology and back into digging individuals based on whether or not their actions were ethical or unethical. And 'ner one of us never ever forgetting nor overlooking that this system, founded on white favoritism, inevitably resists challenge to that fundamental affirmative action, especially when Johnson's involved.

Experience teaches me that the truth and tall tales resonate with more depth, raise more eyebrows, call out more amens, when they fly out the mouths of different men who've embraced their distinctions and individualities. We all got Johnsons. They've all demanded our focus, as we have awakened from boyhood into the roles, actions, expectations, and rites of passage – sexual, emotional, interpersonal, administrative – that mark our journeys into manhood.

We've all been born into an age when Johnson (not a cock, not a penis) shoulders the weight of history, myth, stereotype, and taboo. We all respond to that weight. Sometimes, it's with graceful commitment to a simple, unique humanity. Other times, we calculate based on peer pressure. We pantomime so predictably that we become the punch lines of Richard Pryor's progeny and the scenarios of so-called 'interracial' pornography.

Yet here is what's trippy:

Johnson Chronicles are full of grace, calculations, pantomime and laughter, because we all live with (and within) all that complexity and much, much more. Our love affair with Johnson takes us to places where it gets downright epic, where we have to hold Johnson in our hands, we have to cradle him. Since he is so intimate, so fragile, yet so essential to pleasure and procreation, when we hold him, it feels like we got the whole world in our hands. Truth is, holding him, we cannot lie to ourselves. Autobiography demands we get right.

Aw yeah, but in the telling, Johnson get to stirring. Trickster that he is, he expands in our trembling hands,

Johnson Chronicles

flooding us with power. He reminds us to sneak a twist into our telling. Braid in a trill. Leap from bravado to falsetto. Next thing you know, we got a tall tale on our hands.

    Seeded by just the facts ma'am!

    Watered by the rumble of folklore vibrating along the lines of our blossoming palms.

Truth. My Penis. Tall Tales

Johnson Chronicles

Perfect Fit

From jump, I might as well own up: I got a small penis.

If you tuned in for Myth and Bravado, forget it. I mean, when I'm soft, my stuff sits like a baby chick in the nest of my hairs, propped up by my testicles. If I'm cold, I shrink until I can hide bat and ball between my thighs, and you can't tell whether I'm male or female. I am the cat no man wants to be when the insults start flying:

Baby Boy.

Snickers Bar.

Junior.

I am guilt by association. Be seen with me, and every manhood joke is on you, every woman who lowers her head when we pass might as well sit on the Supreme Court.

Most men just as soon say they can't get it up at all, before admitting they ain't packing no weight. They come up with diseases don't even exist, before they admit they got a little joint.

You know you can hear a dude clearing his throat, speaking conspiratorially:

"It's this *Danglelitis*...."

Or sounding like Bootsy Collins:

"Aaaaahhhhh, just a little case of *Droopzilla* baby!"

Or breaking it down like a fast-talking hustler:

"Like, nah Dog, nah nah: Dr. say, like, all I got? ... A bad case of *Soft Tissue Syndrome*..."

Then then, like he's trying to school a youngster, he breaks it down with an echo of Farrakhan from the podium at one of the Million Marches:

"See my brother if you had ever contracted *Sickle Dick Anemia* ..."

Somebody better call the Centers for Disease Control – quick fast and in a hurry – or we about to have an epidemic on our hands!

Listen, anguish about being soft and hard probably

gnawed at Frederick Douglass, whose dignified testimony echoes across the years. I've seen those Black History Month Facebook posts:

"It is easier to build strong children than to repair broken men."

That's at least a hip t-shirt! And provides more guidance than a motherfuckers's all-purpose demand to man up! I mean, Hip Hop bravado got mugs in Slovakia sagging and flashing Crip signs! Underwear advertisements bulge off billboards. A boy fall down, bust his head to the white meat, he get shouted at to hold back his tears. Can't cry at nothing but the death of your mother! Or in war or after losing a fucking football game.

Saturated by these and other more subtle signals, grown men up the volume on first meetings or peacock across a dance floor or hug a man (not to mention tap him on the ass) only when he wearing a uniform.

Yeah yeah, I know some of the swagger come from Survival of the Fittest and whatnot. And some of that asstapping come cause some of us like tapping that ass.....

But orientation aside, and getting to the big picture of what it has meant being a man, we got to peacock all the time – until the dimension change up on us.

Like, what's the right walk when you roll up into a job interview or a serious business meeting? Check in with your P.O. Assume the position after Officer Friendly order you out the car. How big is big enough then?

And all gavels aside, what's the perfect size and width and flow when you behind closed doors with a lover? What if you actually got a big Johnson? Is your whole life all about what you can do with it? Is Johnson the only companion you need? Sex. Love. Intelligence. Religion. Mental Health. Spiritual fulfillment. How does a big dick lead to a good life, whole living, happiness? Is a big dick that only gets hard when you pop a pill better than a modest joint that gets (and stays!) hard enough for a lover to work through all the Kama Sutra options until

Johnson Chronicles

that satisfied shudder comes down? Ask a mug whose swelling prostate can barely let him pee, let alone get it up on demand.

Frankly, I know it's all good, however many inches make up a brother's endowment. Yet sometimes, on the real, I can't help feeling that somebody else got some of my inches, too, you know. I can't help wondering what deal them motherfuckers cut to corral snips of my DNA to go along with theirs.

Here I am years from junior high school and I am still susceptible to refereeing between the teenager inside me and the grown man who knows better, even though for the most part I'm at peace with my penis. We have come a long way together, if long is the correct word. I am officially standing up for and on behalf of my Little String Bean who tries so hard to be normal. Who tries so hard, hmmm .... Who tries with such determination to represent his sacred place in the gene pool.

When I ain't tripping, I am sure that I'm one of millions of men with penises that don't cast shadows like that blimp flying over the Super Bowl. I'd like to think that it's our time brothers! Think about it y'all, there are way more small penises on earth than there are dolomites. I'm convinced that we need to start our own marketing campaign. Starting with our advantages in lovemaking. So like, yes, it's true that when we're with our lovers, we ain't exactly got them gasping at the very chore of the thing, but they do know we can fit anywhere without them having to go through Lamaze Classes. Ain't no opening we can't ease into and fit comfortably.

Two flashbacks for y'all...

She asked me: you ever tried anal sex?

I was in my mid-20s and the thought was still kind of nasty to me, if I got to own up about it. I hadn't looked at, or touched, a woman's anus. But she was so beautiful. Flawless brown skin. Shape carved from fantasy. A voice distilled from a gospel choir. Big powerful hands that positioned me exactly where pleasure was divined.

Actually she was so out my league I was overwhelmed that we were even having sex, and by that moment so turned out that I was game for anything. Plus, just to put it simply: she had a perfect ass. I already loved kissing each cheek.

"You want to try?"

She stroked my growing joint.

"I like it but it takes the right size and the right attitude."

She stroked me some more.

"I can tell you are big enough for me to feel it, but small enough that I don't tear."

Tranced out, I nodded and bobbed ok. She lay on her belly, spread her legs and arched her back so her behind pouted upward, hands spreading her cheeks. I almost fainted. Turns out, the anus, well ok, the right anus, is gorgeous, and way prettier than I thought it was.

When she guided the head of my Johnson inside, I took the deepest breath of pleasure. Suspended above her like I was levitating ... my arms trembled ... my Johnson beyond stiff, but totally in her command....

"Yes...yes...now eeeeasssee in a little at a time...slowly...slowly..."

I was all the way inside when she exhaled, "that's a perfect fit, baby."

And believe it or not, another lover flat out told me she had sworn off men with big dicks.

"There's deep, which I love, but then there's too damn deep! And I only want a baby up in my womb, not a motherfucking periscope!

Hmmm hmmm.... Small Enough to Deal could be our motto!

We of the Tribe Who Makes Small Tents, lol, should have our own talk show. Call it "Perfect Fit!" Where we can speak our truth. I'm as good a host as any, too, because my very name, to some folk, is a dick.

Johnson Chronicles

Until the birth of that show, I'll just testify and spin this truth and these tall tales. Ideally, it would be interesting to interview men, my gallery of brothers, about their penises, like Homegirl Eve Ensler did to inspire women to talk candidly, and passionately, about their vaginas. But I cannot imagine creating a space safe enough for such an exchange, even though I've helped create settings in which men have discussed their fears about getting married, their pain after breaking up with lovers, and their journeys as dudes trying to be true to the best of their upbringings and conditionings and experiences walking this American earth.

No doubt, though, I'd love to be a part of such a setting, in which we brothers could document honestly and sincerely how we get along with our penises. I don't mean a whole lot of proverbs and tales about size and skill and how many lovers and when and where and in what position and how long we stayed hard, unnhh unnhh! No reactions, nor responses, to any lingering myths of our masculinity.

I mean Johnson Chronicles: simple truths (yeah, ok, some lies) from dudes who've found a workable intimacy with one another, within a setting that cultivates candor and exchange, where worry about being laughed at doesn't define the moment.

By the way, Johnson is the first euphemism I ever heard describing a penis when I was growing up in Southeast Washington, D.C. (Johnson, strangely enough, also happened to be a common last name in my neighborhood, which is a total non sequitur, I know, but it cracks me up just the same!)

To my memory, I never heard the men in my life use the word penis to describe their penis. I never heard them call their penis a cock. (In fact, I was taught that a cock was what white boys called their Johnson, or was the word that described a woman's vagina, when the all-purpose pussy wasn't being used.)

Johnson — cats always sounded like they were on a first-name basis with theirs, you know, and you would swear they were certainly also saying Mister Johnson. Which, of course, meant "I got a big Johnson," and it's a prize to me, a prize to any woman lucky enough (able enough) to swallow him…. Yeah, that's Mister Johnson to you.

I wasn't at all glib, once I entered adolescence, the Testing Time, when Johnson became damn near the only topic of discussion. Before then, my penis basically didn't exist for me, beyond being a part of the body like my nose or my fingers.

In the Testing Time, though, my Johnson was way too small for me to be talking any trash. It wasn't circumcised. If I took a shower and got caught up in a draft, it shrunk up even smaller, like it was scared and retreating back into my body.

Besides, I was an athlete, too, and I spent too much time around young men on baseball and football fields, basketball courts and in locker rooms, to go around spinning yarns about how much my pants bulged. Man, in the Testing Time I wore my towel around my waist so tightly, I could hear Scottish voices whispering in my ear that I looked good in a kilt.

I finally learned, just from showering in locker rooms from junior high into college and on into adulthood, that most of the trash talkers had Johnsons sized just as modestly as mine. Anyway, once I started getting some, and learned that the best sex starts and ends with chemistry, not with equipment, I have learned to cool out and smile at the truth of that saying I first heard standing outside of a Southeast D.C. senior high school:

"It ain't the size of the ship, it's the motion of the ocean."

That truth has set me free. With pride, without stuttering, these are my Johnson Chronicles, simple truths (and some tall tales) about a simple penis.

Johnson Chronicles

Truth. My Penis. Tall Tales

Johnson Chronicles

In The Morning

... In the morning ...
... A three-word prayer ...
... Yes yes yes ...

My Johnson is perfect in the morning. It works so well that if I'm lying on my back, covered by store-bought blankets, I can look down and see a well-supported tipi. If I'm lying on my stomach, if my boy had arms, he could do push-ups so it would look like I'm levitating.

In the morning ... since puberty, that's been like a magic spell, you know, unless you had a stroke or diabetes or something, which I know is serious business and all, but just bear with me for a minute, because, for real, an early morning erection is worth praising.

Feel me! At dawn's early light, when I slide my hand down to embrace Johnson in full bloom, whew, I can imagine up for the down stroke decreed from heaven. I'm throbbing like a didjeridu. Like the echo of God snoring. Full. Firm. It is a flesh & blood gift. If my lover want me in the morning, ain't nothing to it but to do it. I am the want and satisfaction come alive. The Good Humor Man – with my hat turned backwards and the promise of fulfillment ringing in our ears like bells on my ice cream truck.

Man, that's why I love being a dude. Cause we will see the best-case scenario, whenever our Johnson is involved. Especially given how easy it is to go soft – you know: stress, bad diet, child support, noticing my gray-haired reflection in the mirror, hearing about another unindicted police shooter of a Black Life Didn't Matter!

Nothing worse for the AM libido, nothing redefines impotence more, than waking up to the news of a Tamir Rice or Eric Garner or viral video clips of cops exercising some sick dick-over-dick authority by shooting a brother holding up his hands, or running away from the barrel of a loaded gun. Snuff videos, that's what they are, with soundtracks bleeding with historical echoes of mob violence, and of course they sour my prayer.

... In the morning ...?

Then again, wisdom suggests, pledging allegiance to pleasure, healthy pleasure, must be a part of any true antidote to social viciousness! In the worst times, waking up with a hard Johnson, reminds me to make the social moment sweet again. Reminds me, well, basically, that if I can get hard, then once again I'm breathing after (even during) the nightmare. I'm alert, full of life. I get another day to participate fully in this journey, and I can find pleasure, should seek pleasure, on this journey to ensure justice.

Plus, back to the facts about an early-morning hard-on, physiological truth be told, it really ain't even necessarily connected to arousal. The only reason I wake up so hard? I got to pee.

Here comes the sun, I'm easing out of dreams, my mind says hold up boy don't you dare pee in the bed, floods Johnson with blood, switches on that mighty sphincter muscle, and, bam, you got a Love Tool strong as a Black and Decker.

But that biological interlock is truly one of a brother's loveliest sexual ironies. I mean just to keep from peeing in my sleep, I get to wake up with an erection fit for the Let's Get It On Hall of Fame. You cannot tell me nothing then, especially if I'm sleeping next to somebody with whom I can take it to the bridge.

I look over at Homegirl, and I swear, she could be snoring, drooling, and counting so many sheep their wool is making her sneeze, but me and Johnson will be nudging, you know. We will be leading with our hips, announcing, uh, make that, insisting, she shift and receive, even if it take a few minutes of easy in-and-out for her to fully realize we have arisen.

Oh and under the right rhythm, she dial in real fast on what's happening and push me on my back, pausing just long enough to pray in gratitude, whisper to herself

Johnson Chronicles

'Wake up, girl! Wake up!' and maybe wet her fingers to enhance her own flow, before throwing her shapely leg over my hips, gliding into position just above my head, hovering in arousal a few beats longer to further liquefy the moment and drive me officially insane, before sinking until she has swallowed every skin-pulsing inch of a Johnson so eager he bobbing like Ali in his big-mouth prime.

This is when I marvel at the symmetry of our bodies. When I feel her dance inside, waking up to the growing whisper of give-and-receive, Johnson get even harder, each cell straining like in its own private yoga session.

… In the morning …

It's about the only time – for me since I was nestled in my 20s – that I can damn near stay hard for as long as I want. I've even had a lover fall off me in exhaustion (or irritation) because of the gift of this stubborn morning erection.

Of course, on some mornings I've also had such an overwhelming urge to pee that I just can't hang without first heading to the potty. Even if sis is nudging me, and whimpering her invitation, even if her body promising so much give it up, the bed is trembling, the sheets are starting to smoke, and we both responding to that special fragrance of anticipation, I got to go! Even sex got to wait, and you know that violates every code in the *Brother's Hound Handbook*. But I've learned that even if I give in, and try my loving best to do that do, I wind up having to jump up and dash into the bathroom.

Which is worse?

Turning down a begging lover or saying yeah, only to stop abruptly and risk the loss of groove?

Now that's some to be or not to be for your ass!

I have tried to have my cake and eat it too, believe me. Sights and sounds of somebody who already move me (or else she wouldn't be sleeping next to me in the first place) waking up with a jones for me will lead to some sex, it's just that simple. If she want me inside her, and she has spoken or otherwise signaled that I have permission to enter her, then I will enter her. That's just some kind of physical law, you know. Sexual Physics. You don't need no Beautiful Mind to figure that shit out.

Check it, though: a bonafide need to pee will still cause your ass to withdraw. Cause if peeing in the bed by yourself is, like, a zero on a scale of one to 10, then ... well, you feeling me. So there you go: when it reach that critical moment – to pee or not to pee? – most lovers I ever had will agree to me pulling out.

Some mornings, having chosen to brave the bathroom's cold tile in my bare feet, I have wound up peeing with such power, and for so long, that the splash became a drone and lulled Homegirl back to sleep by the time I tiptoed back to bed. Spell is broken when that happens.

Or how about this: One time while I was peeing, I glance behind me and she standing in the bathroom doorway doing her I gotta go dance. That's when we got to open *The Sacred Book for Haunted Lovers*, where there's a whole section on bathroom etiquette. According to how tight y'all are, you got some options.

If it's a relatively new thing, she standing there wearing a shirt, and waits till you finish, not feeling totally comfortable enough for y'all to pee together, even though y'all have been stroking for, say, a few months, after, say, about another four months of minuet.

If y'all got some history, she will be standing there naked and might just crouch in the bathtub if you taking too long. No trip, there, right, cause it's like that, when you got over a year being lovers under your belt. Plus way in the back of your mind, where the teenaged boy is shocked, you know that some warm water will tighten up a bathtub that's been so baptized.

If y'all are stone partners, not only will she appear

Johnson Chronicles

at the doorway butt ball naked, she might roll up beside you at the toilet and swing her shapely leg over the stream you got flowing. Then, while positioned so you can finish peeing right between her legs, crouch in front of you to take care of her business. The Sacred Book cautions us against too much familiarity smoothing some of the sexual edges between lovers, but it also counsels us to keep open for familiar situations taking on their own sexual downbeat.

So, like, there is baby with her back to me, both our streams harmonized, our bodies balanced so that muscles are straining, and next thing you know ... and you know you dig somebody when you actually start getting hard while you peeing!

Oh oh oh! Johnson firm up like it's the first minute of a new day all over again. Here come Marvin humming in the back of my mind, and I slide my hands around her curved hips, and she get the message and she get aroused again, so that even dabbing dry with toilet tissue get her shimmering ....

Ain't nothing like cool tile on your skin when you steaming up the bathroom with sunrise still sweating on the walls. Two people thrilled and grateful once again for that special morning gift:

A Johnson full as a tender rocket ready to fly.

Truth. My Penis. Tall Tales

First Go-Round

I couldn't find her pussy.

It was my first go-round. Poised in the dark of a bedroom, sleep was the furthest thing from my mind. Groping to the throb of my 16-year-old Johnson, which previously had only cum in wet dreams, I should no more have been poised before her sex than a hummingbird should be racing a 747.

I was growing out of the final breaths of my childhood. Fingers damp, but more from nervousness than my inexperienced brush between her legs. Galvanized and repelled by the smell of her wetness. Finally sensing – after much kissing and moaning, mouth-on-nipples, and bow-down before the almighty grind – that it's time to get some pussy! At least that's what my boys called it. Knowing that the relentless hardness between my legs was destined to enter this body, demanding to enter this body.

Only, I couldn't find the most elemental entrance our species has to offer.

I knew my Johnson was sculpted by evolution to fit in her vagina. I just didn't know exactly where it was. I'd seen photos of nude women in Playboy and Players, but I hadn't seen a living, aroused naked woman with her legs open, and with enough light to see the wet evidence of a human female inspired by sexual craving.

Trembling in the dark, though, I tried my best to get it on. I pressed my hard Johnson into her ... pubic hair, foolishly expecting to experience a plunging sensation. Instead, I butted gently into the skin of her pelvis. I probed ... well, actually, I poked, trying to find the physical paradise my hormones and Homies assured me was worth all the struggle to speak a galvanizing opening line, all the green-horn begging, all the awkwardness.

I'm poking, trying to swallow the panic that's seeping across my body and softening me where I sure want to stay hard.

I'm poking, conceding in panic-driven thoughts that I no more need to be here than I need the child we could conceive, cause my naïve ass ain't wearing condom the first. I'm up here depending on luck and her experience as an older woman for contraception.

I'm poking, surrendering to the embarrassment, humiliation and the certainty that, because of my lack of experience and knowledge about biological geography, I will never have sex with this person. And because of my teen-boy ego, I will never ask her to help me find her pussy, nor will I get up to turn on the light. And because I hadn't yet embraced sexual wetness and the smell of excitement, I will never reach down into our sticky crotches to guide myself into the sexual home I was in the bedroom to visit.

I poked until, finally, she grabbed my Johnson, with a touch that said calm down, I got this.

She helped me find her pussy.

With two fingers, she eased me out of her pubic hairs and repositioned me into the geometric space just outside her sex. Then she opened her hand until I rested in the palm for the sweetest, time-stopping pause. I could feel, with the triangulation of a hummingbird lining up a honeysuckle blossom, that all I had to do now was fall toward her and I would no longer be a virgin.

Poised in the dark inevitability, I felt her tilt her flat palm so I was angled that much more perfectly for my entrance. I felt her hand curl ever so slightly into both a cradle and a funnel, so that I was rocked and then poured toward her invitation. Excitement nudged aside my panic. I was swelling again and inching toward my mythical manhood. In my teen-boy's mind, there was no manhood without sex.

But what's that saying: youth is wasted on the youth?

My adolescent hard-on was bobbing like a divining

Johnson Chronicles

rod, bobbing, you better bet it, like the all-mighty Mythical Johnson we supposed to all be packing. Yet my super-charged Johnson was like having a million dollars in Confederate money during the OPEC oil embargo. I had no motherfucking idea what pleasure I could feel or give with all that erection.

Even if I'd found the pussy on the first thrust, I still didn't know shit about controlling my entrance, or easing in with the deep deep inhale, dedicated to rolling my hips until I locked into In & Out with her, only to slip deeper into the one-on-one reinvention of sex that happens, when it's way right for the right two folk. I would learn that's how a real man visualizes good sex.

Poised in the dark, with my first lover, all I had on my mind was getting up, getting down, getting funky, getting loose, which I couldn't do, no way shape or form, unless she was gracious enough – or horny enough – to show me the way inside her. Which she was, fortunately. And with a groaning oh, my Johnson was claimed by moisture silky enough that I could push until our pelvises fused.

Now what?

I won't say I just lay there, without any movement, but I will say that for sure I didn't have any real gifts to give. It felt delicious, I knew that. I now had a body memory of the angle I had to use in order to enter a woman's vagina when she was lying on her back. (Other positions? Never entered my mind!) But beyond the literal fact that I was on top of a woman, and that Johnson was inside Vagina, I had no idea how to riff. I didn't know how to play all that was vibrating within my body. I won't say I wished I was somewhere else, but I will say for sure that I didn't have any real pleasure to give.

Stupid as it sounds now, I believed somewhere in my mind that I was supposed to just naturally know how to stroke. You know: like Sweetback? Think back, all the way back, and remember that scene opening Melvin Van

Truth. My Penis. Tall Tales

Peebles' movie when, as a little boy, Sweetback was whipping it on this big, fine-boned, brown-hipped woman, who was hollering and wailing and whimpering. Well, I was 16. Since my most influential sex education came from shit-talking fellow teen-boys, and you know they was all voting for themselves in a landslide, wasn't I born knowing how to do that do? Why was I hesitating? I was in the pussy – the ultimate destination, far as my boys were concerned. I should be blazing my own groove, unleashing the ball bearings in my youthful hips. I should be stirring my Johnson, swabbing, like my mother with a Q-tip, stabbing, like a mutton-chomping pirate. I should have her screaming like a choir of Holy Rollers, thrashing her head in pleasure from another planet, speaking in tongues like a Baptist just up from wading in the water. I should be floating like a butterfly, stinging like a bee, savoring my teen-boy recipe for mastery of this darkened bedroom, this brown-skinned center of sweet sensations. I should be cataloguing each move I make, each of her responses, so next time I could intensify the my my my and prepare myself for all the Lovelies who I know are waiting on my sexual yellow brick road.

Shiit!

This wasn't no movie! Sweetback nor the Wizard of Oz! I wasn't Sweetback, more like Dorothy searching for her rainbow! I was only a teenager with a hard-on. I wasn't a lover. I wasn't hip. I was just five inches into a body, and as welcoming as that aroused body was, ain't no way I was tapping into the folklore of my neighborhood, my culture, my fantasies. That night, I did not hear the soundtrack for the movie with my name in huge, blazing lights.

And what was that buzzing at the base of my spine? Why did I feel involuntarily pressed deeper into her body? How come with even the smallest shudder of her hips it felt like I was uncoiling? This was good but happening way too fast, although I had no way to measure the pace of this initiation. I hadn't even been inside the pussy two minutes and I felt all the liquid inside me melting into her.

Sweetback never came!

I did. And if I lasted two minutes then it's only thanks to the folklore of my passing years and the kindness of 20-20 hindsight. This exhilarating acceleration, all concentrated in the inches of skin she had welcomed into her body, quickly brought this first go-round to a whimpering conclusion.

You know the rest: I rolled off of her into speechlessness. What could I say? I had no vocabulary for this new use of my Johnson. And if I had just become a man, thanks to this punch-the-clock loss of my virginity, well, grits ain't grocery, eggs ain't poultry and Mona Lisa was a man.

Oh, I had found the pussy (with a little help from my friend), but it was only the beginning of the Blues and the glory that came from the triangulation of a Johnson had found the most elemental honeysuckle blossom our species has to offer.

Truth. My Penis. Tall Tales

Johnson Chronicles

Watch My Balls

No balls, no Johnson. Pain in my balls, no hard Johnson. If I'm hit in my balls, even if my balls get hung up on the seam of a pair of tight drawers, then I cannot be stirred by fantasy, prospective phone number, nude lover, bankroll, or booty call full of pre-dawn promises.

Let me tell you something:

I have been inside her pussy, deep as buttermilk in Virginia pound cake, drawling with pleasure, but accidentally crunch my balls against her thigh ....

Or she could be sucking Johnson with the mouth from all that's holy but accidently squeeze my balls just a bit too hard ....

I fall backwards out of paradise so quick I might as well be a priest waking up in a cold sweat from a wet dream!

If I'm hit in the groin, pain is defined by the wave of oh my God! that radiates off my skin. My face crumbles into a tearful frown. I am not crying tears of a clown! And I ain't bowed down out of respect for no country's queen. Lying in the fetal position is not my secret wish for a return to my late mother's womb. I am not moaning like I'm a Fisk Jubilee Singer cause I'm practicing for an audition at the Apollo.

With all due respect for the universe of pain that humans have endured, that humans have inflicted on each other in war, in pleasure, there ain't no more personal pain than the pain of getting hit in the balls. Every man knows that his balls hurt more than his balls. Period. End of discussion. Fuck logic. Fuck trying to explain it. Hit a cat in his balls and it's all over for the most excruciating seconds of his existence.

For the rest of his life he will remember that pain and do anything and everything to avoid feeling it again.

He will snitch. He will betray. He will beg. He will hide. He will crouch and cover his crotch with his bare hands. He will flinch at a dude getting kicked in a kung fu movie. He will empathize with another man.

Protecting my balls has been Job 1 ever since, as a child, I looked down at them dangling, the one on the right slightly lower than his Homeboy on the left. So delicate. My faintest first memory of just how delicate? The whiff of pain when they clinked together as my mother dried me after giving me a bath when I was about five.

But I became, like, a Secret Service agent for my balls once I started playing baseball as a precocious seven-year-old. I had quickly developed coordination and picked up athletic skills from watching and warming up with my two big brothers who played quality sandlot ball. When they'd get dressed in their uniforms in our communal bedroom, I was fascinated when they pulled out their cups ... triangles made of hard, perforated plastic, which they slipped into a pouched jockstrap, and wore so the cup cradled their penis and their testicles. Ingenious, huh?

When they slipped on their uniform pants, the cups left them with a pronounced bulge in their crotches, which shifted during games. That's why they were always pulling at their Johnsons during their games. (And if watching televised adjustments in all sports except golf is any indication, that's why all athletes grapple with their Johnsons ... although if I was playing golf, I'd wear an iron chastity belt around my shit, hard as they whack at that little white ball!)

Anyway, in our neighborhood, me and my friends played hardball on makeshift fields, where bad hops often banged against our bodies. Ground balls hit me in my chest, in my forehead, rolled up my arms and smacked me in the chin. But I was lucky I was never hit in my nuts. Besides, there probably wasn't a cup small enough to fit my little Johnson, so I played and took my chances that I was good enough to catch or avoid any ball headed directly for my nuts.

A few years later, though, all it took was one ball

Johnson Chronicles

against/into my crotch to make me a believer in the Sacred Triangle of Plastic. During one of my Boys Club games in the 13-and-under league, I slid into third place. I was safe, but the other team's third baseman missed the throw from his catcher, and the ball ricocheted off the glove and slammed right into my nuts. I wanted to cry right there lying across third base. I wanted to kill Abner Doubleday for thinking this game was fun. I wanted to call my mommy, take up Nerf Ball, and vomit on the third baseman's spikes.

And I was wearing a cup!

If I'd been hit in my unprotected balls, I might now be a member of the Eunuch All Stars Hall of Fame!

So you know by the time I played college ball at Howard University, I owned five cups. I was subject to pull out a straight razor, if anybody came within inches of my Johnson without wearing velvet gloves and whispering my name like Linda Lovelace. And I was the proud owner of a Lloyds of London insurance policy on each of my sensitive, precious, priceless testicles. (Sike! I'm lying about that policy! LOL)

But seriously, though, once I felt confident my cup insured my boys, I relaxed and experimented with, let's say, my cup-wearing fashion sense. Mostly, I wore my cup directly over my naked balls and Johnson, then wore long sweat pants during practice, or my uniform pants during games. But in the interest of more comfort, and more protection, I started wearing a regular jock strap on my balls, to lock them in place, then wore an extra-large cup over that, and then put on my long pants.

The most comforting under-laying arrangement wound up being a pair of cut-off sweat pants over my jock, then the cup covering the cut-offs. The jersey material of the cut-offs cushioned my skin against the sweaty strap of the cup, and kept the cup's strap from rubbing against my sweaty skin. Ingenious, huh?

When those D.C. springs got sneaky and turned

really hot and muggy, and we had to trudge off to practice, that's when I became, like, Ralph Lauren. I slipped on my jock, pulled up my cut-offs, strapped on my cup, and – without wearing my long-legged sweats – headed out to the field looking like a freaky-deaky member of George Clinton's road crew. Even my freaky-deaky teammates – whose lewd talk on our road trips in a second-hand Greyhound bus could make Sweetback himself blush – up there claiming they didn't want to be seen out in public with me. Called me nasty. Said I didn't have no home training. Should be booking a room at Saint Elizabeths, D.C.'s home for the mentally ill. They said my mother would faint if she saw me. My daddy would disown me. I needed to be baptized. Or arrested. Walking public sidewalks wearing my underwear. Said I might as well be streaking.

Aw yeah! The 70's!

But listen, I informed every one of them: I'm three times seven, it's too damn hot out here, and I will be looking out for my balls. Then I'd knock-knock on my oversized cup until I heard Ike and Mike, tucked safely inside hard plastic, say "s'awright" like in them El Kabong cartoons. And if I turned a few heads, well, the conservatives could kiss my ass and my fellow freaks say heeeeyyyy! Plus I knew that what's conservative in one decade would be old hat come the next one, so I waved my freak flag high, practiced like a true athlete, and never once worried, cause keeping Heckle and Jeckle safe trumped protocol anyway.

Did then. Does now.

No balls, no Johnson. Pain in my balls, no hard Johnson.

If you a dude (straight, gay, bi, celibate, adolescent or old as dirt), if you a male of the species (and you got a penis, you jack off, scared of it, or think it's God's gift to tight jeans) and your mantra ain't no balls, no Johnson – then you ain't never been hit in the balls.

Johnson Chronicles

If you ain't never been hit in the balls – and I mean hit so hard your voice race from a Barry White growl to a Michael Jackson squeal to a sound of pain so high a dog whistle say fuck it and start barking! – then I'm speaking Spanish at a Ethiopian family reunion and using sign language to a bro whose cataract surgery just been done by a crack-head seamstress.

But if you have been hit in the balls, then you know, oh you know! Down in your chromosomes, you know! In the wet darkness where sperm open up their eyes, you know! In the brain stem, where thoughts are off limits cause you tapping sensations scooped from dirt at the intersection of monkey and homo sapien, you know there ain't nothing to say except three motherfucking words:

Watch my balls!

Truth. My Penis. Tall Tales

When Johnson Gets Blue
"A Hard Dick Has No Conscience."
Says it all, don't it?

It's got the rhythm of the swoon that heat and excitement can well up below the belt. It's got the bragging rights when the rite of passage is being able to answer yeah when your Homeboy asks, "You get in them drawers?" It's got the sociology summing up what we think in the thrill of the moment and what the world says about the self-control of men. It's the Brother's Mantra for whatever takes place behind closed doors – with whoever he with behind closed doors. The excuse from God. An erection that don't enter somebody's body? A waste of God's gift. Wasted energy. Wasted hard-on. Which is the biggest waste of all.

Quiet as it's kept, though, it ain't nothing but the main ingredient of the Blues. Go head, buy into the loss of self-control, the surrender, the teenager's A-OK. A hard dick better have a conscience, or the fallout be more radioactive than a notion, or the fallout play Blues guitar better than Jimi Hendrix.

I bet y'all don't think we ever say no to sex? Cannot believe any dude with his parts in working order has ever stood before somebody – whose whole body pulsating – and yet still said no. You'd call me a stone liar if I told you I have lain beside a naked woman and realized that saying no was better than sliding into wetness. Listen, there have been times in my life when I have turned down more sex than the law allow, even when I wasn't with nobody else, and was free to swing to my hips' content. And soon as I insist on having a conscience, or work up enough will power to resist the glaze in two sets of eyes, sex beckons like I been offered every wish I ever felt.

Right this moment, I can remember visiting this woman. We hadn't done nothing yet, but we felt that voltage between us. Anyway, at one point in the visit, she had just stepped out the shower and was sitting with me on the couch wearing only a terrycloth robe. Baby was clean in so many ways: she told me wasn't no lover on the scene, she hadn't been flowing since they broke up, she'd been digging me like an old Marvin & Tammi Terrell duet, and every word she spoke was telling me to come on and let's figure out our real thing. She was holding my hand and swirling her thumb in a circle in the center of my palm.

Yes yes yes .... This was Silver Platter Pussy! Magic Genie Pussy! A Wet Dream to the 10th Power!

But ... I was still reeling from being dumped by somebody I really dug. I forced myself to go visit this woman, trying, you know, to follow my Johnson to the Promised Land. But in the back of my mind I was holding on to my most ridiculous wish. I was pining for a telepathic message to come back home. My inner ear was cocked so I could hear the voice I most wanted to hear. I convinced myself there would be reunion if I just said no to this hairy invitation from a naked woman shuddering underneath her bathrobe.

Looking back, I have kicked my own ass 20-11 times for having a misplaced conscience. I cannot believe that all I did was rouse myself from the couch, raise her hand to my mouth, kiss her fingers, adjust my hard Johnson, and drive back home to my empty house. There was no message blinking on the answering machine.

I can't lie: Right this second, I am haunted by the thrilling memory of her soft thumb softly circling my palm. I can recall the quiet in her house as she revealed how ready she was. Ain't many women willing to take a shower while I sit in the living room. I can still see the sun going down through her window. The clearest case of temporary insanity in my entire sexual lifetime.

Every time I find myself surviving a period of unintentional celibacy, or stinging from the rejection of women who won't let me get a whiff, I am living witness

Johnson Chronicles

to the times when Johnson gets Blue.

Of course, what really brings out the Robert Johnson is our biggest fear: impotence. Especially given how easy it is to go soft – you know …. Lucky for me, I've suffered mostly from temporary impotence, and not a case that need blue pills and implants. I've gone limp because of stress brewed from holding shit in, or getting distracted by my fantasies for some unattainable lover. Or anger. Or guilt. Or lack of money. Or those times when I was just going through the motions and sex was more like a 9 to 5 than a Maxwell love song.

When Johnson softens, and he supposed to be hard, is when two realizations take my breath away. One, without Brother Johnson, I can't do my duty for the species. Take away morality and a hard dick with no conscience may literally let me do my do for procreation. In that sense, I'm bowing down before our genetic altar, when I sow my oats, as my Pops used to call it. I'm heeding the Call of the Wild to spurt as much semen into as many wombs as I've got energy and game to enter!

But, number two, if all I do is hit it indiscriminately, I never learn that sex is God's love song. I am numb to the human ascension from straight animal, the human expansion into sublime masculinity, that happens when I slip into Sacred Darkness with that Lover who heightens the physical into the metaphysical, whose smell, curve, voice, walk, intellect etches every experience into my permanent memory bank. Y'all don't hear me! If all a brother do is fuck a pathway out of his constriction, he will forever stay numb to the inevitable genetic and cosmic music that … that … pulses … when sex grips us, seizes us, and we feel that shimmer, and we know, if we own up about it, we transforming – we are being transformed – from lust to lovers to Loved Ones.

And here's the sweetest irony: When the intimacy is tight, and there's silliness, surprise, mutual respect and interdependence, we become, like, Ambassadors from

Super Freak! We get more funky, more primal. Fearless about why that place taboo. Satisfied by a breath. Cum from a kiss on the cheek. Slip it here. Slip it there. Slippery when it's wet. We get it: Sex is time, and time is God. In a world full of the Blues, we make time for God.

Impotence loses its threat, because we define conscience as recognizing the humanity of your lover, and yourself. Don't matter if you enjoying a quickie, one-night stand, or crying cause you confirming a life-time commitment. Consent forms the clan. Honesty is the dowry. Satisfaction is the vow. A hard Johnson confirms our place in the concentric circle of human passion flowing from genetic obligation and our quest to learn sex's cosmic secret.

Once, like I said, I felt the circle being traced in the palm of my hand and said no. Body pulsating with an erection, I remembered I was looking at a member of my extended family. All bullshit and trash talking aside, I knew I couldn't keep it up. I literally couldn't make the time.

Johnson Chronicles

Truth. My Penis. Tall Tales

Skin Off My Johnson

Any mark on my Johnson scares me. Even though I learned as a teenager in health class the symptoms for every VD known to us before AIDS, and have kept myself aware since then, I'm skittish at the slightest hint of discoloration, change in texture, or twinge anywhere in my groin. Plus, I examine myself like a MD gone mad, even after a physical when test results say I'm so healthy you could eat me for dessert.

But let a mole show up, I swear prostate cancer so far gone it's eating outward and become a pinprick of inevitable death. One ingrown pubic hair cause a swelling, and I shudder like I got a 24-hour appointment for chemotherapy. A deeper red on my already red-bone Johnson after a shower, and I'm scrunching up my face in the bathroom mirror, counting off every lover I've ever had. I worry whether I'm sexually active or weathering droughts that last long enough so that if I did have anything serious it would have long ago shown symptoms. I'm sensitive about the health of my penis, as if it can, by itself, regardless of my overall health, develop, like, its own genus of disease.

Because even when healthy, by design for God's sake, Johnson's duties include peeing or sliding erect into a mouth or vagina or anus, when his skin changes, then I can hear sinister whispers, some round-the-way primal memory from puberty, that dick can die and drop off my body. Leaving me alive with nothing between my legs but hair. In the back of my mind, I can hear my parents, preachers, and teachers. Moms telling me how careful I got to be, now that I'm having wet dreams. Rev. Do Right is telling me, 'boy keep your manhood in your pants,' now that urges glaze my eyes and cause me to get hard just sitting next to a girl. And teachers are warning me that I know better, now that I've learned the dangers of pregnancy and disease.

The hygienic, grown man I am, the selective,

discriminating lover I am, tries to face down the vestigial echoes of my adolescence. But I'm subject to fits, if I examine my stuff and notice any mark that in my hysteria I know, just know, wasn't there yesterday. I counsel myself with common sense: Skin on my Johnson subject to the same variations as skin on my face, my back, my feet. I remind myself that I use only the most organic cleansing bar on my skin. I wash my penis with TLC. Talk to him. Hold him when I sleep. Shake excess urine from his tip, even if I'm at a public men's room and cats rocking foot-to-foot behind me. I examine my boy from all sides, when he soft, stroke and squeeze just right when he hard. I freely drop my pants during physical exams, so the doctor can do his do unencumbered by Fruit of the Looms or my hang-ups. I'm intimate with my penis is what I'm trying to say. I got an adult relationship with my Johnson.

Yet, let his skin feel too dry and I'm maxing out my Amex card on supersize containers of aloe vera gel. Let him have a baby scratch, probably caused by a hangnail during masturbation, and I'm down on my knees praying what I got ain't resistant to penicillin. Discomfort on the first spurt after holding my pee too long, and, oh Lord!, I'm calling the 1-800 number of the National Institutes of Health for referrals to research labs. If the NIH put me on hold, I'm scouring the World Wide Web to catch up on the latest symptoms of AIDS-related complexes.

The skin of my penis has worried me off and on ever since I entered the Testing Time. As I said, that was in the Seventies and I was still, on occasion, prone (well at least willing) to sexing women I barely knew. (Truth be told, I wasn't all that prone, except in my fevered and fertile imagination.) In them days, health issues didn't seem so life and death, so it wasn't no thing to pair with a lady you vibed with at the disco, or at the free sundown concert down at Anacostia Park. Oh yeah, we was into condoms – or rubbers as we called them, or prophylactics,

Johnson Chronicles

if we was trying to sound really hip and medically on time. But even if we did have sex skin-on-skin, we was mostly worried about getting Homegirl pregnant and, at the WORST, running up on a case of syphilis or gonorrhea, which were the two stars of sex education films being shown at the time.

So right about two years after I graduated from high school, I had a surprise visit with an ex-classmate of mine. We'd barely talked in school, but I remembered her because she was this tiny woman who also had these phenomenally large, marvelously shaped breasts. And she fit together perfectly, you know. She had, as the Whispers might sing, the body by Fisher. Right there, talking on the sidewalk, we both was saying, yeah, I remember you, and, right right I didn't say nothing back then, but I felt something, and ain't it strange that two years later, here we are, and would you like to get together? How about later today, after we get off work? And what's your number? And what's your number? And here it go, and I'll call and come by in my '62 Chevy Impala, what?, say around, like, 8 o'clock?

I did arrive around eight that night and in the trunk of my Impala was a blanket, which we wound up using as a bed, laying on the grass over in Anacostia Park. Kissing, you know that. Coveting her breasts, yes, yes, yes, you know that. And more stunning: she was coveting me. She was not shy like I thought she was two years ago.

She did choose to unbuckle my jeans and shake me down, and I was allowed to unsnap the button to her jeans and shake her down, and we did agree that skin-on-skin was worth the risk. And it's true, I only lasted inside her for the proverbial hyperventilating minute of the inexperienced male, but I was inside her, and we sipped friction on a summer night down by the river. No we never saw each other again, which is just about the Seventies newsreel moment.

But it don't stop there: a few days later I pull

Truth. My Penis. Tall Tales

Johnson out to take a leak and damn, there's, like, this rash on the head of my penis! I freak! The rash is shaped like hatchmarks, as if I'd pressed Johnson against a screen or something. Oh shit! I hadn't seen no sex ed film on which we could find references to red embroidery on my dick!.

Now you know I didn't act responsibly and call sis and let her know I had this rash. In fact, for the longest couple of days I didn't talk at all – to anybody. I went all James Bond and shit! Ran through the very limited medical file cards in my head trying to determine if this rash was life threatening or not. (Of course it was life threatening, you idiot, I told myself, cause any mark on Johnson is scary, plus I had just been with Homegirl without condom the first and damn she probably pregnant on top of carrying this horrible disease.)

When I was sure I was going to die and orphan my unborn child, I worked up the nerve to ask my father for help. Which is worth a dissertation itself, because me and him had not so much as winked at each other on the sly about sex. But I needed to talk and I needed my daddy. That summer, he had gotten me a job working on the gardening truck he drove, which gave me the chance during a quiet moment at lunch to, uh, like, you know, ask him about this rash on my thing.

But guess what happened?

Pops heard me out, and then, like he was a colored Marcus Welby or somebody, started asking me simple, thoughtful questions about how I got it, how long I had it, did it hurt (and actually it didn't; it was just there!), until finally he told me to show it to him.

Huh? Show my Johnson to my father? On a lunch break outdoors under some shade trees in a DC neighborhood where our only privacy existed in the shadow of the truck? I mean I'd seen him take a leak – from behind – or I'd seen him step out the shower, but pulling out my rashy penis for his inspection? Damn if this wasn't an off time for a freaky version of Pops Knows Best.

Johnson Chronicles

But damn if the simplicity of his request, the common sense of his bedside manner, didn't make me feel, finally, that showing him my penis in public wasn't the most normal thing in the world. He looked at the rash. He never touched me. But he had me move my joint so he could check out the rash from different angles. I was calm, although my heart raced and I was blushing big time.

Another thing, too:

He wasn't tripping that I'd had sex, and sex without a rubber. Wasn't no moralizing or nothing, although I am absolutely sure (now that I've fathered both sons and daughters) that he was no doubt just as worried as I was about my irresponsibility. It's just that for the moment, in the moment, as we stood in his outdoor examination room, Pops was on a medical mission for his Number Three Son. He could have easily been wearing a white doctor's coat, a stethoscope around his neck, and rubber gloves, instead of his Monday-Friday work clothes. Finally, after his inspection, he looked me in the eyes and said:

"Did you pull the pussy hairs apart before you did it?"

Whoa! This was a question from another sexual galaxy. My answer was no, of course. As a way inexperienced and newly minted 20-year-old, I was just so happy to be near the pussy, let alone having this beautiful, excited young woman pulling me into her pussy, that I pushed forward as fast as I could. Pops explained that's why I had a rash as if the head of my penis had been pushed against a screen.

"Her hair must have been real thick," he said. "Next time, spread her hair apart before you do it."

He said not to worry. The rash would go away in a few days. It did. It did. I wasn't going to die. My dick wasn't going to drop off and leave me with a hairy black hole between my legs. Pops never said how come he knew so much about parting hair. (And I sure wasn't imagining him and Moms about to get down!) It's a mystery I never solved, since he died before I could revisit this particular memory of ours. I never got to ask if he had learned from his Pops how to prep a wanting pussy so as to avoid a rash or pregnancy.

Looking back, I know now that me and Pops missed a chance to get closer faster, after he'd schooled me during that lunch-time diagnostic session. After all, I've never had another rash, which means he was like a colored Marcus Welby. And I have parted my share of hair, which is truly another story, since that led to the very satisfying habit of actually making serious eye contact with the pussy, and having my own personal vagina monologues....

Well, at least now maybe I've cleared up why noticing any mark on my Johnson drives me crazy. As much as I monitor myself, as sure as I know exactly where my Johnson's been, you let so much as the wrong light fall on my boy ... I will squeal for my father like I'm Butterfly McQueen on steroids.

Make me want to pack my penis on ice, until Ebony.com features an ad for that special cream could smooth away wrinkles, even out my complexion, and soothe the brow of the late adolescent still fretting in the heart of this skittish grown ass man, who still wishes that he and his Pops had gotten even closer, after he schooled me on a hot, humid summer day, when I showed my father the skin of my Johnson. We did bond over the years. We did. But we could have saved ourselves even more distance, you know.

That 20-20 hindsight thing haunts me. It haunts me still.

Johnson Chronicles

Truth. My Penis. Tall Tales

Johnson Time

Once I saw the subtle, wise, pioneering comedian Franklin Ajaye talk about how when God was making a man and woman he got to the genitals and paused. God frowned in concentration and wondered how to ensure procreation. Aha, said God, reaching up into His Heavenly Storage Bin, and pulling out a few nerve endings. God stitched them into the penis and vagina, then paused again in thought.

"Nah, that ain't enough!" and then dumped the whole bin full of nerve endings into the primordial Johnson and Vagina.

"I want them to scream my name," God said.

All that hot wiring has transformed my Johnson, lo these eons later, into a divining rod. In fact, I read that it's actually my brain that gets turned on by a sexy sexy, that the real chain reaction begins in my gray matter. Ignited by a fragrance, a curve, a voice, a walk, even an intellect, and within nanoseconds Brother Brain is signaling my pulse to race, my pupils to dilate, my nostrils to flare, my hair to rise on my neck, and finally my penis to twitch or get erect.

Science may have documented all this, but it feels like my Johnson is the brains of this operation.

He jumps to attention so fast in the right presence I know my penis got its own independent power source. I can be distracted – say by worry or work or I'm on the subway reading – when Johnson just jumps to his J-O-B and I know that glancing up I will see a distinctive woman glowing. My question to the lab rats is always this: If my Johnson is responding, then is Homegirl flashing, too? And if she is, shouldn't I say shyness or protocol be damned and step to her?

Oh God, I pray to embrace my Inner Johnson.

What good is having such sensitivity if I don't cultivate the creative eloquence I need to speak up and really determine whether it's simply molecules racing or if

Truth. My Penis. Tall Tales

I've truly received serious signals from a potential lover? What freedom rides a rising penis? Since I'm sure that I ain't a true hound, and I do have the discipline to say no, why not be confident that I'm only genuinely excited by a woman who's bringing it in some genuine way? She might be signaling that I got the look. She might be pulsating at my fragrance, my curve, my voice, my walk, even my intellect. She might be poised to swing into conversation should I respond to our mutual unspoken shake and bake.

Crossroads showered and electrified by immediate sexuality, reduced even for a classic hot minute into juiced nerve endings, paralyzes every part of me but my Johnson. I sure can't think straight. I have felt surging enough times to know that I cannot inevitably say something that acknowledges magnetism, yet doesn't sound so raw that I'm porno when I should be flirting, you know.

Quiet as it's kept, in Johnson Time, you ain't got but a nanosecond to harness the chemistry, sort the signals, balance boldness and hesitation, decide if it's mutual, weigh the social setting, determine potential consequences, and hide your erection, before opening your mouth. To my thinking, only a straining penis could reach out with certainty within such vibrating calculations. Maybe a physicist who's at the top of the intellectual food chain, or a consummate player constantly swooning to classic slow jams from late night TV ads playing in his mind, could adjust Johnson and speak on it with savvy.

But me ... I either revel too much in the throb or punk out with a cliched aw shucks she couldn't be fiending for me. I swear I can hear my Johnson sucking his teeth when I waste all the energy he's channeling. I can hear him say, see, you always whining how I ain't got no conscience, that I done got you in enough trouble, and here I am guiding you to goodness, trying to help a brother on the really real. Look at her! Trust me, she's got the look. Her *shekere* is simmering with the rhythm meant just for you! It's handled my man and you up here thinking

Johnson Chronicles

so much I'm losing my power.
      Then as my penis gets soft, I can hear him whining like that witch in the Wizard of Oz.
      I'm meltiiinng…!
      Johnson Time.
      You snooze, you lose.

Truth. My Penis. Tall Tales

Johnson Chronicles

In & Out

In the Intimate Church of Johnson, the sacrament is friction, the manna is rhythm, and the faith is in the immaculate instance when the stroke is so rock steady death and life are measured by the In & Out – the disappearance and rebirth along the glistening length of my excited erection.

Aw yeah!

I was mesmerized the first time I truly noticed the exquisite slip and slide of my penis during sex. I was so in the pocket that I opened my eyes. I was hypnotized by the delicious perfection of parts that fit so profoundly. It was absolutely riveting. My excitement possessed my body. My Johnson intensified into a supple stiffness, a sustained straining. I entered a calm awareness that we were generating holy sensitivities, and that our hum was inviting us to get comfortable with escalating pleasure, because our stroke had already banished distraction. All we had to do now was revere the In & Out. That first time of my witness, I was on top of my lover. But, no doubt, I have reveled in receiving, with a lover kneeling and rising, or crouching and rising, and the gift is the same, regardless of position. The hide-and-seek of my penis welcomed and released by my lover is beyond intoxicating.

It's Church.

Of course, it's all good – literally speaking – whenever Johnson meets Sally. But it's no question that the sacred swooning I'm talking about ain't on the program with everybody. Cannot be planned. Cannot be talked up. Cannot be promised. Cannot be bought. Ain't no guarantee you'll see In & Out, if your partner's round the way or hincty. Red bone or jet black. Little. Tall. Sister or white girl. First-time lover or old flame. Ain't no guarantee if you stroking in the A.M. or in the first minute of the new day. In your own crib or a five-star hotel. Stroke speed don't matter. Cannot bang your way In & Out. Cannot hit it or think in any way shape or form of

Truth. My Penis. Tall Tales

Johnson as a weapon or tool of submission or emissary of ownership.

Got to supplicate to bow at the altar of In & Out. Got to be human and singed by the one you with, hungry and called by the human with whom you fit. Got to be open to the roar of Teddy Pendergrass and the siren of Minnie Ripperton. Got to love Johnson as, like, a wick of incandescence, attraction and passion. Must want to be where you are, with your mind off your money and the what ain't? The who knows? The coulda woulda shoulda. Must know who's loving you and love her smell, her touch, her air. Must love your own body. Must love hers. Must be prepared to laugh. To well up with joy at the sheer ump ump ump of In & Out. Get happy at the improbability that two complex, complicated folks choosing to be together and are matching movement, connected by instinct and improvisational pleasure, doing it as only they can. In & Out is all y'all's, and can only be y'all's, and, aw yeah, will only be y'all's, even if goodbye or get out my face are on the horizon, and silence rules the rest of y'all's lives.

In the immaculate, regenerating instance of In & Out, all that's honorable is the magnificent fit that's magnifying and elegant and wiping out the everyday and sinking us into delicious union. I now long for In & Out. I kneel for the laughter come more thrilling than climax, waves of grateful laughter more exciting than heavy breathing and whispered testimony. Hope to see my throbbing Johnson slide till my tip kisses her cervix and we mesh pubic hair, then, then, then glide back into view till I'm poised to fall out, but never fall outside her liquid gravity. I supplicate to In & Out, over and over, till into the air around us gathers a mist of our voices, silence and knowing that seeps into us and gives us permission:

Honor the friction. Ashe.
Be a slave to the Rhythm. Ashe.
Hold to your Faith. Ashe.

Johnson Chronicles

    Now go on…get down.
    Aw yeah! Aw yeah! Aw yeah!
    And don't stop, please don't stop, till you get enough.

Truth. My Penis. Tall Tales

Johnson Chronicles

Praise Song

Wrestling with taboos minted in my adolescence, if not fully banishing their echoes, is how I've come to an elemental peace with my Johnson, how I've come to accept him, and feel, yeah, he completes my body. Without investing Johnson with immutable power and consciousness, as if he existed – could exist – as puppeteer or bully or Alpha Peer outside my control. I'm thinking of taboos like once I'm hard I got to fuck. Echoes warning me, don't get naked unless you taste it. Taboos in which it's all about me, my nut, me getting off, my satisfaction – circumstances be damned, opinion and permission of the woman be damned. As a father of daughters, grandfather of granddaughters, and as a '70s dude always on the lookout for humane self-development, it's gotten easier to draw a line from these taboos to what's now called Rape Culture.

But, ironically, I've come to believe the biggest taboo for dudes is way more personal, way more me myself and I. The biggest taboo? Digging masturbation. I mean really celebrating the touch of my hands on my penis. One finger tapping the opening at his tip. Two fingers squeezing the center of his throbbing erection. Gripping the entire shaft and squeezing waves down his length and up my spine until my body shudders and drops of semen leak into view. Sliding my hand, slowly, then faster, then slowly, accelerating my breath and regulating the growing excitement, knowing I could come, holding back ejaculation, until touch and thought and fantasies convulse and pleasure shoots into my hand, onto my stomach, and into my brain. (Or is that the other way around?)

I ain't saying that masturbation is taboo on GP.

I know that cats masturbate.

But if my earlier life is any example of the impact of the taboos, then we don't actually pleasure ourselves. We jack off, you know, jerk off, visit Miss Palm and her five daughters. We grab Johnson and whip away that

Truth. My Penis. Tall Tales

tension or strangle our frustration, but only when we ain't fucking or we're otherwise missing out on sex with a lover.

I've come to feel that the taboo is against really grooving on solo sex, even when – especially when – you hooked up, got a lover, getting some, loving somebody, want to be with who you be with. The taboo demands that I only grab my penis when I absolutely have to, not cause I want to revel in the sensations I can conjure by stoking my Johnson in the magical privacy of my own time, in my own mind.

The taboo orders us to take our hands off of ourselves. Orders us to go out and buy some pussy if we can't talk up on none. And if we can't beg none, we ain't manly from the git, the taboo sneers, so we sure can't find our manhood pulling on our own thing.

I'm fighting that limited view of myself. Pleasuring my Johnson is more than spurting and going to sleep. Savoring my Johnson is more than releasing tension. It leads to satisfaction as complex as the celebration women have permission to tap when they pleasure their own sex, with its folds and centripetal configuration and moisture and fragrance. And I for one ain't hating on what women can find within themselves. Shoot, I've been known to kneel before the female labyrinth and use my fingers and tongue and nose and psychic open sesame to see (if not climb) all the way to the womb.

But by learning to celebrate the mystery of my own sex, I have become mo better at seeking my place in a woman's vagina, and, most worth celebrating, I have neutralized the reverb of the taboos transmitted to me by the more braggadocios aspect of becoming and being a man.

So, with no shame in my game, this a straight Praise Song to my Johnson.

I'm taking a bath. Hands soaped and hidden by bubbles. I'm washing my Johnson. Washing. Not seeking

Johnson Chronicles

the convulsion. Washing my Johnson and cupping my balls with slippery hands, as I squat in the water. Rubbing soap into my hair. I'm soft. It's sensual but not sexual. Stretching foreskin and circling soap around the crown. Lifting him and stroking suds underneath. Lathering up some more, opening my thighs, sliding wet hands into the angles of my crotch, working back to my penis. Grabbing tub's edge with my left hand, I raise my pelvis and flatten the palm of my right hand on top of my relaxed Johnson. Pressing down the shaft with cleansing strokes. I ain't in no hurry. Look down at my boy and he smiles in gratitude that I'm washing him with love, and with more than hygiene on the agenda. He holds his breath as I sit with a splash back into the water to soak away the soapiness. I wiggle my hips to separate shaft from balls, swish the liquid warmth into the soft folds of my scrotum sac. Run some more hot water into the tub. Turn off the faucet. Take a deep settling breath. I am satisfied for several expanding moments, enjoying the sound of the water lapping against the sides of the tub. Then I soap and rinse the rest of my body, pull the plug and stand up.

    Water falls from my clean Johnson. I start drying off by tucking my penis and balls into my towel. Homeboy is like a terrycloth mummy for a minute. The water soaks into the cloth. I slide the towel through my legs so I can dry my anus, before wiping water off the rest of my body. While standing before the mirror in the medicine cabinet, I moisturize Johnson first. It's become a ritual now. I want his skin to be the softest on my body. I figure he's the most vulnerable part of my body. He should be at the center of my TLC for myself. Lather up my brother to make sure he's tender and then rub the excess into my hair and down between my legs. It used to be bad taste to leave the house with ashy legs. I can't leave my crib now unless I'm sure my Johnson's skin ain't ashy, and is moist enough to weather the several times I have to pull him out in public bathrooms.

Truth. My Penis. Tall Tales

My secret's out.

By making sure that Johnson is pampered for his daily J-O-B, I practically guarantee that he's up for his more sensual work, when I stroke him myself, or when a lover holds or kisses or swallows him. I stay excited knowing my man is Ready for Freddy. I love to feel Johnson growing under my touch. Love the rush of thrilling movement inside that matches the exploration of my fingers, my palms, my nails. Love how he throbs after reaching fullness, bobbing erect from my body, emanating an invisible field of sensitivity. The air against him excites me. My thoughts become fantasies – old lovers, women I touch with my wishfulness, women who have said no and ain't studying me no kind of way.

I'm excited by doubts that I shouldn't be excited. How could I be sitting or laying up in here fondling my Johnson, when there are real women I'm attracted to, real women whose bodies I want to touch and enter? Lingering with myself, liquefying myself, I'm sinking in these conflicting sensations. Finally, me and Johnson focus on the simple fact that we feel good and ain't no stopping us now. I'm in the privacy of my own crib, where I pay the bills (surely my father's fundamental definition of manhood). I ain't shouting to a lover, "Whose pussy is this? Whose pussy is this?" (though I've begged that question once or twice and heard my name in the air). I ain't putting my hands on nobody without their permission (confident there ain't no sex without consensual sex). And I'm free, Black and over 21 (just to make sure a taboo-monger know and know I know, you know!).

And when Johnson speaks and sparks and sparkles, I feel like a man's man, handling all my business. I'm always ready to share my thrill, but I'm never again surrendering my right to go for what I know. Stepping with Johnson as my Homeboy. Clean as the Board of Health. Grown as a Chicago Bluesman. Fortified as a

Johnson Chronicles

secret know it's been told.

Truth. My Penis. Tall Tales

Head

My lover's eyes are glazed beneath her fluttering eyelids. She slides down to her knees in front of me. She has me propped up on the soft, plump cushion of her comfortable chair. She has my legs spread and bobbing against the thick armrests. Her eyes are riveted on my throbbing Johnson, my straining Johnson, my whimpering Johnson, my Johnson with a teardrop of cum seeping from its center. It's not the first time she's savored my erection with a gaze so full of my my my! It is not the first time her look promises authoritative touch. But it feels like the first time. I feel like I am the finest man alive in the lull of her appreciation. Down on her knees, she leans toward my penis, her mouth a welcome oh....

Minutes ago, I was wearing silk long johns. When I took off my jacket, the sight of my hard nipples through the fabric thrilled her. She bent to kiss each nipple. She grabbed the waistband of my jeans and pulled me toward the chair in the corner of the room. The belt melted under her abracadabra. She shoved me into the chair. She untied my shoes, unraveled me from my pants.

We are stripped of all protocol. She is in charge. She bites her bottom lip at the sight of how excited she has me. She pinches my stinging nipples through the silk top, which she has left me wearing. My hips twitching, she inches my Johnson into her wet mouth, flicking the sizzling tip as she swallows me. She sucks my skin with perfect pressure she knows I love. Not too hard, but not too soft. Claiming me, but giving, too, you know. Enthusiastic, but subject to strolling, too. Her whole mouth calibrated by a tongue know how to test, tease, taste, then table any doubts about what's in store for me if I behave, if I trust how she translate her excitement, if I let her seal her groove.

I nestle into the chair's creases. I open my mouth to breathe, only to release a moan that's a Mantra of Gratitude. She bows in her own prayer, and her moan and her pressure and her pleasure and her joyfulness ripple from her mouth along my fullness. I know her mouth. I want to kiss her kissing me, but she keeps me locked where she wants me by pressing her palms hard against my chest.

Be patient, her hands demand. Lay back.

This mine.

She cups the base of my Johnson with one hand. She sucks me down her throat, holding me more rigid than I thought possible, then draws back until the tip sits between her barely parted lips. She laps me. She milks me. She turns me in slow circles, stir it up, opening and closing her mouth in a liquid *reggae* against the tip of my Johnson. She moves her hand back to my chest. With both thumbs, she caresses my nipples in time to the in-and-out, up-and-down motion of her mouth. When she slips both her hands beneath my ass, I'm already arched upward. Her hands only confirm the obvious.

This mine.

I don't argue. I swell. I dance. I defy gravity, floating on her magic tongue slicing down the length of my Johnson until she's sucking each testicle with the tenderness of a virtuoso wine taster.

Who named this kiss head?

Such a little word for touch which stops time, when it's on time. Having a lover's mouth mother my Johnson separates me from my body, focuses every cell in my body, and celebrates the power pleasure brings to my body. Such a little word for touch that wrings electricity from the wetness of taboo, risks the concentration of cum and saliva, swears on the satisfying tension between a kiss and a bite, and confirms that we trust pleasure over pain.

Head cannot capture the exhilaration of hearing her say hmmph hmmph hmmph as she lifts off my Johnson just enough to glare down at my ringing body, at my thrashing body. Head cannot describe the sound of her mouth returning to find the perfect suction, rising and falling, rising and falling. Can't capture the richness of her delivery, her giving. Head can't describe the groan shuddering from her mouth spiraling down to her own sex, as she settles down to the unmistakable mission of claiming my climax if it's the last thing she do in her life.

This mine.

I like to kiss her right after she swallows. Savor her tongue, taste myself, taste electricity from the wetness of taboo. Taste the concentration of cum and saliva. Swear on the satisfying tension between a kiss and a bite. Confirm my trust in pleasure over pain.

The kiss is gratitude and confirmation that I love myself, that I know myself to be healthy. Whatever you can have in your body, baby, I can have back in mine. You ain't taking no more chances than I take myself. You kiss me, you drink me, you quench me, I kiss you, I drink you, I quench you. No part of my body is a threat to you. No part of your body is a threat to me. You crave me. I crave you. I excite you. You excite me. I am irresistible to you. You magnetize me. You nourished by my smell, my waters. I inhale your fragrance, your humidity. You volunteer to suck my Johnson. I volunteer to kiss you right after you swallow.

Head cannot even wade into such deep waters.

Head will drown in such deep waters.

Such a little word for what is at its best her praise song to my Johnson. A song can sound like the blues of a street-corner singer, the purr of Eartha Kitt, or the whimper of Etta James on her third encore. Taking my Johnson into her mouth is a gesture that all at once blends her passion and confidence and control and surrender. At the same time, having my Johnson in her mouth intensifies my excitement, shoos away any doubts about her desire, inspires me to lose control, and demonstrates my surrender.

Down on her knees, leaning across the stick shift in the car, crouching before me as I stand against a kitchen counter, sneaking under the covers in the first minute of a cuddle after a hard day, sliding up and down like a child on a candy cane, cradling me in the satisfying silence of skin-on-skin, or blowing a regretful kiss at an early morning erection when the rush to work won't allow us to get all the way down – mouth mothering Johnson will lead me to show her the truth of the proverb my father taught me:

Fair exchange ain't no robbery.

Johnson Chronicles

Vasectomy

A vasectomy is not castration, but try telling that to your Homeboy. No matter what you say, there's one nut he just cannot crack. I mean, you go all out to ease his worries. You tell him the operation is the hippest and best birth control on the planet. He say Ok Ok. You tell him he never has to worry, ever again, about getting nobody pregnant. Right right, he say. You tell him that after a vasectomy you and your honey can put the spon in spontaneous, you feel me! His eyebrows raise with serious interest on that one. Plus you swear on your mother's grave that coming still feel the same – you just don't release no sperm in your semen. Cake and eat it too, he say. There you go, you tell him. If you don't want no kids, or if you already have as many kids as you want, then the Big V is definitely what's happening. But then he ask, like, exactly? How …? You know. What get cut? Where does the cutting get got!? And before you can get your description roll on, it's over, because there's that one nut he just cannot crack:

Using scalpel and penis in the same sentence.

Homeboy's face look like Kunte Kinte when that axe is up above the overseer's head. Black men just got damn near a genetic aversion to blades near naked skin. And Homeboy is not hearing no stories about initiation ceremonies in Africa neither. Trekking off into the backwoods with all your puberty partners, so you can get turned on to how to be a man, what to do with women, how to hunt or provide for a family, you know, getting tight on the village history and customs and codes and all that. Only to top it all off by submitting to a circumcision? With a sharp edge wielded by one of the old brothers? And only some plants and shit to numb up Johnson? Or whatever they call your penis in whichever language the elder praying in while he slicing and dicing? No sir buddy! Homeboy say, brother, I will just have to be, like, an honorary white boy or Asian, or somebody. I am not having sharpened stainless steel next to the most sensitive skin I got. Unnh unnh! It ain't happening.

So there you go: even though a vasectomy is the hippest birth control out there, you can see that it's a really really personal decision.

But I had one. And if ever I get so fortunate as to earn me a lover who wants to stroke everyday, then I could get up on the down stroke everyday! Yes yes yes, we could put the spon in spontaneous. And looking back on my decision to cut my tubes I'm still mostly sleeping well at night.

Check this: It's 1981 and I'm lying on the operating table at Howard University Hospital in Washington, D.C., about ready to have a vasectomy. I am 25 years old. You hear me! 25! Even the doctor, a brother, asked me before the surgery: "Are you sure? What if you want to have a child? This is irreversible, you know." I told him I already had a son and a daughter and was helping to raise another daughter I had adopted. I had contributed enough to the gene pool and now it was time to have some sex without worry. (I sure didn't see the AIDS clouds boiling on the horizon.)

But it was more than craving worry-free sex that had me sitting with Brother Doctor. Much as I loved the kids I had, I was already so overwhelmed it's a wonder Johnson could work at all, even one in the prime of his 20-something life, even one that could get so hard he'd yank me in the direction of a sexy woman walking past me on the sidewalk. I had embraced my children. I liked them. I was all up into being a good daddy, too, changing diapers, giving them baths and dressing them, rocking them to sleep on my chest. Fathering with imagination, you know, reading them stories, always trying to make them smile and feel loved and wanted. I was 25. I felt like a hundred and five. Boxed in. Needing money. All the time. Tempted by all the fine women who cooed at me when I was out strolling with my kids. Barely stirred by their Moms.

Johnson Chronicles

I was probably suffering from my own postpartum Blues. But didn't, wouldn't, ask nobody for help. Thought I was supposed to lie in the bed I'd made. Blueprint already set: you hang, do the right thing and be sexually unfulfilled, because you worried all the time. Or you split – worst case you split and never look back. Best case: you split because in your depression you open up to some new woman and, like I did, ignite the cycle of baby mama drama. Or you see having a vasectomy as an option, a way to trade some temporary pain between your legs for a future of sex whenever you and yours got the feeling (and can find time between work and taking care of a son and two daughters).

And that's how Brother Doctor wound up being my surgeon. Come to think about it, my surgical team was a Pan Africanist's delight: a sister from Ghana was my anesthesiologist and a Trinidadian woman was my nurse. Thanks to local anesthesia, I was awake throughout the operation. We actually laughed a lot, since I kept up a running monologue with one basic message to Brother Doctor: do not slip and cut the wrong thing.

See, I know intimately why my Homeboy got the jitters. In fact, after the doctor had finished my surgery, and sealed off the pathways my sperm followed in order to be ejaculated, I ordered him to show me the two pieces of my vas deferens. Actually, it's really scalpel and scrotum sack should be in the same sentence, cause the surgery calls for cutting into the flappy skin on either side of your balls, not the skin of your penis.

Irregardless (oooh my Moms hated that word!), I admit you must be serious if you want to have a vasectomy, especially back then, when it was truly considered an irreversible procedure. Only once did I wish I could reverse my decision: after my inability to have children frustrated this woman who said she really loved me. When she left me to have a child with another lover, I was so broke up I researched the state of microsurgery to find out how possible it was to reverse a vasectomy. (Man, talk about closing – or should I say opening – the barn door after the horses had all bolted in a stampede!) Eventually, I went to Kaiser to attend a course for men considering having a vasectomy, so I could ask about a reversal operation. When I found out how expensive it was to pay for – what should I call it? – a *Vasattachment* operation, and that it ain't covered by health insurance, well, I chalked up that love affair as the one that got away, went home, got butt naked, and said to my Johnson: 'OK, bro, whenever I get over this heartbreak, and you start getting hard again, just let some sex be in the mix. Somebody in for some sheer spontaneous pleasure.'

So, how did a cat educated in the Round-the-way Sexual Academy, come to the conclusion to block the flow? After only about ten years beyond puberty? Turns out my oldest brother was the first person I knew to have a vasectomy, and he inspired me to have mine. He didn't want any more than the two children he and his wife were raising. He wanted to relax sexually. By the time I laid under the knife, in all honesty, I was so scared of accidental pregnancy that I didn't even think I was making an out-the-box or radical decision, even though I had to fight through my own urban Black boy's genetic aversion to stainless steel on my naked skin. Finally boiled down to being more afraid of having more babies than I was of Brother Doctor slipping while he was leaning over my pelvis.

But after it was all over, and once it was clear I could still get it in, I dug how genuinely free I felt, you know. I knew the truth of what the women writers I was reading and meeting were saying about owning your body, controlling your sexuality – for political and personal liberation. Having a vasectomy demonstrated my seriousness about parenthood. I was saying that if I was going to be taking care of kids, then it was going to be the children I already had. And I will not lie: it felt so good to

Johnson Chronicles

know that I couldn't slip or be tricked into having a child. My manhood would be defined by responsibility, not biology.

After the surgery, when I was wheeled back into the recovery room, I was certain I was heading into a teenaged boy's paradise – sexing anybody I wanted without worrying about pregnancy. I know better now, after facing other, more emotional, consequences. I regret that I couldn't make a family with someone I loved. I occasionally wonder if one of the millions of sperm I've blocked and consigned to reabsorption by my body contains the secret inspiration hungered for by the whole planet. What if I was supposed to be the father of another hero to take the place of those game-changers who got assassinated right before our eyes?

My Pops used to tell me you got to take the bitter with the sweet and he ain't never lied!

I think my Homeboy senses all this, all worry about castration aside. He knows that a vasectomy is the best birth control, and I know he would love to have his cake and eat it, too. I know I can't tell him what he should do. It's too serious for that. He'd have to feel it right where his bones start growing out the marrow. Snipping out a part of his reproductive system should be taken seriously. If he feeling the right circumstances, though, I'll even do stand-up comedy in the operating room, just to keep Homeboy relaxed, and so I could watch over his surgeon's shoulder. And you know my monologue will have one basic message:

Do not slip and cut the wrong thing.

Truth. My Penis. Tall Tales

Johnson Chronicles

Pops and Them

Which way to get My Fathers up in here?

It's much more mysterious than just replaying the first time I saw Pops naked, or talking to him about a particular sexual question or dilemma. Although I was shocked and genetically gratified to discover that he, too, was part of my diminutive tribe. And over the years until he died, it was cool to find that whenever I came to him genuine, then he'd come back at me with sincerity, commonsense and insight.

But when I think about My Fathers – Pops and Them: the gallery of older men I've known – I think of a strangely soothing link to a bunch of jazzy cats who lived hard-working lives. They were modest for the most part. Their talk of sex and references to Johnson were sly, laced with innuendo and flooded with the subsonic appreciation of deacons, who channeled their youthful passion into style, substance and simplicity.

Makes me think about cussing. I mean, it turns out my Pops could cuss his ass off, but I only learned of his expanded vocabulary of profanities when I turned 18. Where before, he'd say son of a bitch or shit or damn in front of me, once I got legal, I started hearing him say the same words that I'd been saying with my boys outside the family home. My shock was only equal to my naivete.

But now that I'm way way grown, I seriously miss Pops and Them. My Fathers. My dead fathers. When I think seriously about life, I do think seriously about my Johnson, because so much of my life as a man is charged by sex, getting some, or not getting none, or making the right sexual decisions.

I imagine Pops and Them as guides. I see them all sitting at a big round poker table, with my father as HSIC – Head Spirit in Charge. As suave as they were in public when they were alive, that's how laid back they are in their rec room in paradise. I see them wearing white sleeveless undershirts and suspenders clipped onto paisley boxer shorts. They wearing tie-up wingtips and over-the-calf thick-and-thin socks. They sipping one round after another of some brand name liquor and chewing unlit cigars. They reach into their drawers to adjust, fondle, or maybe just laugh at their penises, which by all rights they don't even need no more. But that's how I see these dream merchants, these embodied memories, these ancestors shaped out of prayers I float during the running soliloquy in my head.

    I thank them when I get an erection. I thank them when my erection excites a lover. I thank them when I make love. I itemize to them the qualities I'll want in my next lover, when my current lover leaves, or after I choose to move on. I can hear their voices, rising and falling, exquisite signifying possibilities and mixed signals: well …, and er ah…. Their voices are an overall soundtrack that never provides specific steps I should take, but which always sound right on time.

    Since I'm especially trying to live in harmony with my Johnson, I seem to really be begging for their long-winded ruminations, whenever I'm grappling to find my balance between a hard dick and a soft behind. I meet more than my share of women who excite me and have Johnson licking his lips for a dip. He bobbing and stirring and daring me to find words for his cravings. Homeboy is so persuasive.

    I consider My Fathers part of my resistance to Johnson's indiscriminating call. Even if, like I said, Pops and Them still tax my patience, with their own catcalls to 'go head and get you some, boy, because we see your future, and you better roll with it now, cause you in for a very long wait.'

    Rolling my eyes, I wait until they remember they're only fondling ether in their boxer shorts. Once I weather the ripples of their residual humanity – which is what you get from ghosts personified as randy Black men from D.C. – they come through with best-case, worst-case

Johnson Chronicles

scenarios, as I'm standing and talking with a sexy woman. They may shout RUN, if it's clear that I'm on the radar screen of a drama queen. They may mumble half-and-half if Homegirl got potential. They've even been known to ignore me altogether, and up the volume on their card-game insinuations, cause they know a man mostly has to take chances and make choices on his own.

My Fathers, despite clinging to their lost humanity and its quirks, predilections, and appetites, have proven to really have my back when I'm suffering the backlash of missed chances or heartbreak or droughts during which I'm getting to know Johnson way too intimately. I say proven like this a science project. I mean I am comforted knowing that when I look inside and peep my wisest get down, I'm staring at a mythic reflection wearing round-the-way haberdashery, sounding off with neighborhood eloquence, and sealing my wounds with sensations kept under wraps until they know it's time to hand out the biggest bowl of cobbler.

Having Pops and Them as metaphysical advisors soothes my intensity when I'm feverish. They help me ID the integrity when I'm famished, rip through the protocol when I'm feeling it toward somebody. They are never an amen corner. They remain as ornery and cantankerous as saints, as they were walking the sidewalks of our lives. But they are always available.

They just don't want to give it up too easy. They want me to work for the Right Thing. Which is the least I should expect of spirits who sit around in their underwear, sucking imaginary teeth, scratching imaginary balls, and adjusting imaginary Johnsons so their bulges don't show too proud.

... And, quiet as it's kept, they know the skeletons in their own closets can make even a ghost bite his tongue, fail you in life and fail you in the afterlife!

... Some memories burn like embers in a bassinette.

Truth. My Penis. Tall Tales

It was second-generation abuse. First my sister, and now he was overheard slurring something nasty at my pre-teen niece, the daughter of his daughter. Trying to poison the future!

Aw hell no! He wasn't excommunicated the first time, when I was a teenaged witness. Now I was in my early 40's, a father of daughters myself. Bite my tongue now and I become one of the elders who leaves a child standing in line for love when lightning strikes the crossroads.

I called up my brothers, my sisters, second wife (thank God Moms was already dead!) for a family meeting at the dining room table, where we'd all sat at Thanksgiving, at Christmas, on his birthdays. No hesitation in my voice:

What the fuck are you doing? How many times we supposed to forgive you? For the first time! This shit is over! This ain't my house but I will take your key right out your motherfucking pocket!

He cried. Agreed to counseling. Apologized. Blamed it on that vodka. Broke everybody's heart. Again. Still human. Still Pops. Still had five years to live.

A month before he died, we sit in a car outside the first house he and Moms ever owned. Rain soaked the streets. Tears soaked his face. Siren glaring from the fire station around the corner. Or was it the police?

My Dead Fathers.... Can I revere them in all their humanity? They didn't always fondle ether in their boxer shorts. Some of them hurt people. Some of them poisoned the future. Some of them never said I love you. Dangled their Johnsons before their children.

I need to believe that in the afterlife they've heard echoes of Coltrane's A Love Supreme or Mahalia's Somebody Bigger Than You and I, and risen above the sorriest common denominators of their lives. Forgiveness, which don't ever come easy, can seriously be a full-time job! Pops and Them, My Fathers, Dead and Gone Ones,

Johnson Chronicles

are now beyond judgment, but still exercise such influence over the everyday.

Don't need you to be an amen corner. Just don't ignore me. Help me recognize what's left of the best you still have to offer. It's me, your son, standing in the need of prayer, clinging to your lost humanity, your flawed humanity, and its quirks, predilections, and appetites. It's me wishing you would really have my back when I'm shaking wrongs out my sheets! When I'm suffering in the backwash of all your humanity.

Can you still comfort me?

Can you be my mythic reflection dressed in round-the-way haberdashery and sounding off with neighborhood eloquence?

Can you still comfort me?

Truth. My Penis. Tall Tales

Mythical Johnson

Haunted by Pops and Them, ain't nothing left but to come correct with my simplest truths. So, for real, I ain't hating on cats with big Johnsons. Only hoping that whatever the size of his Johnson, a mug is using his joint without staining nobody's future. And that we all can be at peace with the real skin we got. I have my flashes of doubt, which I own, but I know my little partner is packed with all the erotic sensitivity and biological imperative he can handle.

No it ain't the physical I'm wrestling with right along through here. It's the metaphysical. I got my Mythical Johnson on my mind, and my mind on my Mythical Johnson. The one that's so big that all Black men got one.

Yeah right!

First off, saying that all Black men got a big penis ain't no more a compliment than cracking a yo mama joke. May make for funny punch lines, and there really ain't much funnier than a good Big Dick or yo mama joke. I have laughed at the best of them for years.

But on the DL, the compliment is connected to a whole 'nother collection of subsonic He said/She said:

All we care about is hitting it, all the time.

Can't spell love with a gun to our head.

We the poster boys for lust.

Rather have a white woman than bathe.

And we really more gorilla than man anyway, with the brains to match.

Each myth go way way back…. This history's cold … and it's deep, too!

Alright then, when did the Big Black Johnson come to mean I ain't human?

The answer, which is over a thousand years old, is first mystical and theological. Then it becomes anthropological and political, until in America it becomes the national assumption, the racial obsession, and even the proud cultural assertion.

Homework shows that my Johnson was targeted by the (supposedly) smartest minds that the so-called civilized world had to offer. They found me lacking, and ended up splashing way too much testosterone on the pages of treatises and travel journals and rationales. Slavery, for example, then colonialism, for example, were explained as good things, civilizing and indispensable, because I was the voracious, lascivious, shameless missing link between all that's animal and all that's white male.

Guess what wound up happening?

We've all been spooning from a gumbo of ideology dressed up like science. It really wasn't nothing more than ruling-class gossip, humor, and signifying. Backed up by the force of guns, intellectual hocus-pocus, artistic stereotype, and drylongso that come from living with ideas that have simmered, shimmered and silhouetted the boundaries of our psychic matrix from the 1600s to the 21st century.

"The idea that black sexuality – and the black penis in particular – was sinful was an invention of the Judeo-Christian tradition," asserts David M. Friedman in his book *A Mind of Its Own: A Cultural History of the Penis*. In Chapter 3, 'The Measuring Stick,' he writes: "The source for that linkage was the Bible, where the battle between good and evil often took place between a man's legs...."

"But where do blackness and large penises enter the picture?" Friedman asks. "Some experts, point to a passage written approximately seventeen hundred years ago in the Midrash, a commentary on the Old Testament that is one of the central works of Orthodox Judaism...."

Quoting the translation of one of the commentaries in *Hebrew Myths: The Book of Genesis*, Friedman says Noah ends up cursing the descendants of his son Ham, who saw Noah naked:

"...Because you neglected my nakedness," the commentary has Noah saying, "they shall go naked, and their male members shall be shamefully elongated! Men of this race are called Negroes; their forefather Canaan commanded them to love ... fornication."

Friedman breaks it down further. He says that although this commentary is "lacking any standing as Jewish law, out of several million [words] in the rabbinic writings, [it] had an impact on Western culture its author neither envisioned nor intended."

Why?

Because medieval Europeans consolidated their belief in the bible as the "Word of God," as they were exposed to this message through biblical translations by monks who had learned Hebrew.

"The subsequent convergence," writes Friedman, "of three events – the arrival of Europeans in sub-Saharan Africa in the fifteenth century, Gutenberg's invention of the modern printing press (circa 1436), and the resulting publication of the Old and New Testaments in English, French, and German in the sixteenth century – meant that more people were reading about the Curse of Ham just as more Europeans were meeting his '"descendants."'

So what happens?

"The biblical meaning of the black penis," as Friedman puts it, gets "fixed" in the minds of "self-proclaimed experts," who bet the imperial farm on the equation:

Big Black Dick = Less Like Human!

In 1607, for example, a dude named Edward Topsell could write in his book, *The Historie of Foure-Footed Beastes*: "...Men that have low and flat nostrils are Libidinous as Apes...," according to the book *White Over Black: American Attitudes Toward the Negro, 1550-1812*, by Winthrop Jordan.

In 1735, Swedish botanist Carl Linnaeus, in his *Systema Naturae*, for the "first time included man within a complete classification of the natural world," asserts Adam Lively in his book, *Masks: Blackness Race & the Imagination*.

Linnaeus included the following description:

"African. Black, phlegmatic, relaxed. Hair black, frizzled; skin silky; nose flat; lips tumid; crafty, indolent, negligent. Annoints himself with grease. Governed by caprice."

In the nineteenth century, it got straight hysterical. French colonial army surgeon Dr. Jacobus Sutor, wrote:

"In no branch of the human race are the male organs more developed than in the African Negro ...," Friedman reports. "It was among the Sudanese that I found the most developed phallus, ... being nearly 12 inches in length by a diameter of 2 ¼ inches. This was a terrific machine, and except for a slight difference in length, was more like the penis of a donkey than that of a man."

Whew!

But get with this: Before my Johnson got zapped by civilization's high priests of rap, all cultures tipped their mythological cap to Big Boy, without playing all that pin-the-blame-on-the-penis.

I mean, ever since we pimped away from being Homo Habilis into Homo Erectus and on into Homo Sapien, and riffed until we evolved distinctive cultures, Big Boy has been part of a functional society's respect for the power and mystery of procreation. He was respected as symbol of the male's contribution to keep on keeping on, just as folk bowed down to the almighty home of female sexuality.

"Egyptian worshippers of Osiris and Greek worshippers of Dionysus carried unmistakable ... representations of erect penises in their processions – and they knew very well that they were engaging in phallus worship...," writes Susan Bordo, in her book *The Male Body: A New Look at Men in Public and Private*. "...The phallic images that Osiris worshippers carried in their processions ... were signifiers of rejuvenation and sexual

Johnson Chronicles

pleasure...."

Since ancient times in Africa, our species' Briar Patch, Big Boy has lived a long life of reverence! That's clear from the text and, especially, the photos published in the 1964 book *Black Eros: The sexual customs of Africa from prehistoric times to the present day.*

For all of humankind, through the ages, Johnsons – huge, symbolic Johnsons – were painted in bathhouses, sculpted into folks' cribs. They adorned pottery, were carved into statues, found on musical instruments, included in people's religious rites and ceremonies, and just overall appreciated as a natural part of life and living.

Which is a trip to me, because my Black Johnson – culturally and socially speaking, that is – ain't been revered in no way shape or form. When I was born in 1955, and left D.C. General Hospital with my little uncircumscribed joint, I was unknowingly wading into and saturated by the legacy of the equation that say me and my kind were better breeders than citizens.

Mythologically speaking (work with me, now), my Johnson has only been divine when it benefits somebody's bottom line. Mostly, it's been devilish and, too often, cause for MF's to go shouting and shooting and gathering under strong limbs of strong trees to watch a brother swing and burn and be castrated. All based on the Old School Big Johnson myths.

Man, my Johnson sent folk into an erotic trance.

"Mandingo men were 'furnisht with such members as are after a sort burthensome unto them,'" Winthrop Jordan quotes Richard Jobson, who Friedman describes as "a bible-quoting, treasure-hunting Englishman who spent several sweaty months exploring what we now call the Gambia River in West Africa."

In 1623, Jobson wrote a book, with a title longer than any Johnson on record: *The Golden Trade: or, A discovery of the River Gambra, and the golden trade of the Aethiopians. Also, The Commerce with a great blacke Merchant called Buckor Sano, and his report of the houses covered with Gold, and other strange observations for the good of oure own countrey; Set down as they were collected in travelling, part of the yeares, 1620-1621,* by Richard Jobson, Gentleman.

Jordan quotes another cat from 1665, the "anonymous author" of *The Golden Coast*, who wrote that Africans were "very lustful and impudent, especially, when they come to hide their nakedness...." The term nakedness was a euphemism for penis, according to Friedman. This traveler gasped at the "...extraordinary greatness..." of my Johnson.

"Negro men sported 'large Propagators,'" according to John Ogilby, another 17th Century traveler quoted by Friedman, who reminds us that "...reports of preternaturally macrophallic Africans peppered European travel writing once Portuguese ships landed on the continent's western shores in the early fifteenth century."

"...Indeed, the idea antedated the settlement of America and possibly even the Portuguese explorations of the West African coast," Jordan writes in *White Over Black*. "Several fifteenth-century cartographers decorated parts of Africa with little naked figures which gave the idea graphic expression, and in due course, in the seventeenth century, English accounts of West Africa were carefully noting the "extraordinary greatness" of the Negroes' "members." By the final quarter of the eighteenth century the idea that the Negro's penis was larger than the white man's had become something of a commonplace in European scientific circles...."

That's when my Johnson, to hear Jordan tell it, became epicenter of a dangerous ritual – castration. Cloaked in the official rationales of science, sanctioned in the legislated ceremonies of government.

One of the founders of anthropology, Johann Friedrich Blumenbach, wrote:

"...It is generally said that the penis in the Negro is very large .... And this assertion is so far borne out by the remarkable genitory apparatus of an Aethiopian which I have in my anatomical collection...."

Wrote the English scientist Charles White in 1799:

"...That the PENIS of an African is larger than that of an European has, I believe, been shewn in every anatomical school in London. Preparations of them are preserved in most anatomical museums; and I have one in mine."

"...The white man's fears of Negro sexual aggression," Jordan writes, "were equally apparent in the use of castration as a punishment in the [English] colonies." Legislators from the Caribbean to New Jersey authorized my castration for "striking a white person or running away" from enslavement.

Even as "gradually rising standards of humane treatment for all human beings tended to limit the use of castration as slave punishment," Jordan writes, "... as late as 1758 North Carolina authorized its use, and until repeal in 1764 the colony was paying jailers for performing official castrations and reimbursing masters whose slaves failed to survive...."

That ain't all:

"... Castration ... was reserved for Negroes and occasionally Indians ...," Jordan writes. "In some colonies, laws authorizing castration were worded so as to apply to all Negroes whether free or slave. ...The Pennsylvania and New Jersey laws passed early in the eighteenth century (and quickly disallowed) prescribed castration of Negroes as punishment for one offense only, attempted rape of a white woman...."

"...Still more strikingly," adds Jordan, "Virginia's provision for castration of Negroes, which had been on the books for many years and permitted castration ("dismemberment") for a variety of serious offenses, was repealed in 1769 for humanitarian reasons, but the repealing statute specifically declared that it might still be inflicted for one particular offense – rape or attempted rape of a white woman...."

Jordan concludes:

"...Castration of Negroes clearly indicated a desperate, generalized need in white men to persuade themselves that they were really masters and in all ways masterful, and it illustrated dramatically the ease with which white men slipped over into treating their Negroes like bulls and stallions whose 'spirit' could be subdued by emasculation. In some colonies, moreover, the specifically sexual aspect of castration was so obvious as to underline how much of the white man's insecurity vis-à-vis the Negro was fundamentally sexual."

My Johnson, literally, even took on the color of evil.

"... Nearly every European woman burned at the stake for consorting with the Devil described his penis as black," Friedman writes, in a chapter called 'The Demon Rod.' He actually begins *A Mind of Its Own* with a visceral account of the public burning of Anna Peppenheimer, a 59-year-old German mother of three, charged during the Inquisition with the "one crime that virtually all the women confessed to after torture ... knowledge of the Devil's penis."

I told you it's deep.
Ideas sink and seep.
Gossip saturates and situates.
Myths colorize and calcify.
Beliefs intensify and stereotype.
Weapons contain and enslave.

My Johnson becomes a symbol instead of an inherent body part. Intensified until it pulsates with no connection to human arousal, no connection to what is unique about my size, my desire, my fear, my confidence, you know. Like I'm on an auction block, or paraded through the corridors of counting houses, my Johnson is fondled without permission, guided and goaded only by power stolen from deformed definitions of civilization.

Stealing excitement from taboo.
Calculating hipness from fetish.
Signifying superiority until it's mantra:
From Holy Book to Constitution.
Border to border.
Imax to cyberspace.
Cradle to grave.

"The ongoing encounter between white Europeans and black Africans between the fifteenth and nineteenth centuries, a commingling more extensive and intimate than any that preceded it ... transformed the cultural role of the penis and significantly expanded its meaning as an idea," Friedman writes. "This cultural shift was cited by Europeans to justify not only colonialism and castration – those black penises in the specimen jars had to come from somewhere – but slavery on a scale unprecedented in world history. For better or worse, the penis was racialized."

For better or worse? Please! In the Big Picture, vibrating with ugly subsonic whisper, we're left with a straight color breakdown.

Big Black.
Little White.
Impotent Mulatto.

We're left with what Friedman calls "... the fear of the big black penis ... or the belief in its accuracy as a measuring stick of bestiality...."

"Most racial thinkers," Friedman writes, "based many of their most important conclusions on the same criterion – the African's penis. It was stared at, feared (and in some cases desired), weighed, interpreted via Scripture, meditated on by zoologists and anthropologists, preserved in specimen jars, and, most of all, calibrated. And, in nearly every instance, its size was deemed proof that the Negro was less a man than a beast."

Damn!

And this sickening survey only focuses on the

ruinous riffing that backed the nearly 300 hundred years of the Atlantic Ocean slave trade. There was also over 1,000 years of slavery of Africans practiced by followers of Islam, which routed millions of enslaved Africans "across the Sahara, from the coast of the Red Sea, and from East Africa," according to *Islam's Black Slaves: The Other Black Diaspora*, by Ronald Segal. From the year 650 to the 20th century, the number of Africans enslaved under Islam ranged from about 11 million to 14 million, according to scholars cited in *Islam's Black Slaves*. Scholars have estimated that almost 12 million Africans were "loaded onto ships during ... the Atlantic slave trade," writes Segal, who is also author of *The Black Diaspora: Five Centuries of The Black Experience Outside Africa*. The total number of Africans devastated by Christian and Islamic slavery multiplies, Segal writes, if we count the "men, women and children taken or lost during procurement, storage and transport."

Of the Islamic trade, Segal writes:

"One late-nineteenth-century writer held that the sale of a single captive for slavery might represent a loss of ten in the population – from defenders killed in attacks on villages, the deaths of women and children from related famine, and the loss of children, the old, and the sick unable to keep up with their captors or killed along the way in hostile encounters or dying of sheer misery."

There were "two females to every male in the Islamic Trade, and two males to every female in the Atlantic one," according to Segal.

Segal makes pains to indicate that in contrast to the systematic, theological, scientific, and round-the-way signifying that supported the Atlantic Slave Trade, Islamic slavery, "by specific precept and in common practice ..., [was] relatively humane in its treatment of slaves and its readiness to free them, even though individual Muslims have been among the most ferocious slavers in history."

The Koran, Islam's Holy Book, "while upholding

the distinction between owner and slave as part of the divine design, also expressly encouraged the freeing of slaves as an act of piety," Segal writes. He adds that, "for much of Islamic history ... there was no such virtually exclusive identification of slavery with blackness as came to exist in the Christian West with colonial expansion and the Atlantic Trade.... However," Segal notes, "prejudice did promote discriminations. By the Middle Ages, the Arabic word 'abd was in general use to denote a black slave, while the word mamluk referred to a white one."

By the nineteenth century, when slavery under Islam "exceeded any of the previous twelve centuries in the volume of this trade," according to Segal, the human lust for power and territory and profit did lead Muslim enslavers and their suppliers, including African suppliers, "to involve violence and brutality on a gigantic scale."

Yeah, and my kind, the Africans with a Johnson, got dissed in a horribly particular way:

"Unlike white eunuchs, deprived only of their testicles, black ones were subjected to the most radical form of castration ... level with the abdomen ... based on the assumption that the blacks had ungovernable sexual appetite," Segal writes, referring to research by John Laffin, who wrote *The Arabs as Master Slavers*.

Segal reports that such castration actually afforded me with "peculiar opportunities for vertical mobility." In other words, cutting off all my stuff meant I could then be trusted to guard an HNIC's harem, or work as a military slave, or as an administrator for the ruling royal family.

Castration reached its vicious peak during the 1800s, when the "raiding and warfare for slaves were conducted on a scale and with a ruthlessness that seemed at times frantic," Segal writes. Ironically, the pressures exerted by European imperial expansion – which culminated in the 1884-1885 Berlin Conference to divide African territory into European colonies – contributed to the rush for profits. Segal writes that eventually European governments pressured for the abolishment of slavery in their new colonies, which had of course been won through expansionist wars.

"Islamic enslavers, peeping that a change was gonna come, rushed to cash in with a desperate ruthlessness. As the century climaxed, they used "new rapid-fire rifles" during their raids. Often, they killed "many of the surviving adult males who had been injured or were insufficiently submissive for safe transport, while females, especially young ones, and boys were all seized, as these were the ones most in demand by the markets," Segal writes.

"Young boys, in particular, continued to be sought so that they might be turned into eunuchs," Segal writes. "And given the account of how the operation was performed … it is surprising that any at all should have survived."

So, for example, in Bornu, located in central Africa, and which was Castration Central for prized African eunuchs, one leader who sold slaves just went buck wild. He would "collect from time to time hundreds of boys, and … subject them to castration, condemned though this is by Islam," Segal writes, quoting Gustav Nachtigal, a German physician who traveled from 1869 to 1874 through various parts of the African interior and published three volumes from 1879-1889. Nachtigal's volumes included "vivid accounts of the storage and transport condition in the slave trade," according to Segal.

In Bornu, Nachtigal witnessed the impact of absolute power over my life blended with absolute greed:

"Under the pretext of wanting to circumcise the boys, the barbers who performed the operation are accustomed with a quick grip to grasp the whole of their external genitals in the left hand, and with the right to amputate them with a sharp knife. Boiling butter is kept in readiness and poured on the flesh wound to staunch the bleeding of the unfortunate boys."

Johnson Chronicles

Flesh wound? What's up with that? They cut off my Johnson and my balls! And used boiling butter as post-op anesthesia! And sold my ass if I survived my trip to the barbershop? So I could watch over enslaved women kept prisoner so a motherfucking sultan or somebody could have his choice of fresh pussy! Ain't shit humane about slavery! I don't care who quoting scripture, or reading shells, or putting their finger up to the wind to sanction my ultimate impotence. I don't care if they followers of Allah, Jesus, Jehovah, the Great Sprit, Olorun or any motherfucking other divine concept. Keep your hands off my body! Keep your knives off my Johnson!

Shit!

It's easy to see, when it comes down to me and my Johnson, when it comes down to sex and the influence and allure of taboos, why even the descendants of so much racist ruminations and practices would just say fuck it and grab hold of the Big Black Dick, even if they don't actually have one. Listen to The Virtuoso, Richard Pryor. He told one story of cats taking a piss off the Golden Gate Bridge. One dude discovered that the waters of the San Francisco Bay were cold. The other said, "…yeah, and it's deep, too!" Richard even had Andrew Young holding his Johnson in the Jimmy Carter White House, and exciting the First Lady, who tittered, "… oh that's alright. Bigger than a peanut…"

In Pryor's 'Cocaine' monologue on the recording Is It Something I Said? he cracks:

"…Niggers be holding them dicks, too…White people go: 'Why you guys hold your things?' Say: 'You done took everything else, motherfucker!' Nigger be checking!"

> Laughing to keep from crying.
> Tears out the eyes of Dolomite!
> Once you go Black….
> But liberated by the laughter.
> You never go back!

Lifted beyond the bullshit by the laughter.

Two more points to hit it and quit it:

About that gorilla comparison? Turns out that the "length of the erect penis is only about 1¼ inches in gorillas ... but 5 inches in humans, even though [ape] males ... have much bigger bodies than men," reports Jared Diamond in his book, *Why Is Sex Fun? The Evolution of Human Sexuality*. Diamond says male gorillas ain't macking, either: "Even male gorillas with a harem of several females get only a few sexual opportunities each year; their mates are usually nursing or out of estrus."

Plus "gorillas normally ejaculate in one minute," Friedman, in *A Mind of Its Own*, writes in a footnote attributed to Diamond. The footnote continues: "Chimpanzees have been timed at seven seconds. Humans, with an average time of four minutes, are actually among the slowest to climax among male primates."

And it ain't like the news that gorillas wasn't men and men wasn't gorillas didn't make the historical front page, either.

"In 1699, the web of legend and unverified fact was disentangled by Edward Tyson, whose comparative study of a young "orang-outang" was a masterwork of critical scientific investigation," writes Jordan in *White Over Black*. Back in the day, Europeans used orang-outang for all simians except the obviously huge great ape, according to Jordan.

"Throughout his dissection of the chimpanzee," Jordan writes, "Tyson meticulously compared the animal with human beings in every anatomical detail, and he established beyond question both the close relationship and the non-identity of ape and man. Here was a step forward; the question of the ape's proper place in nature was now grounded upon much firmer knowledge of the facts."

Yeah, but folk making big bank off the buying and selling of humans weren't prone to let "firmer knowledge

Johnson Chronicles

of the facts" get in their way:

"Despite their scientific importance," Jordan reports, "Tyson's conclusions did nothing to weaken the vigorous tradition which linked the Negro with the ape.... The sexual association of apes with Negroes had an inner logic, which kept it alive without much or even any factual sustenance.... By forging a sexual link between Negroes and apes, furthermore, Englishmen were able to give vent to their feelings that Negroes were a lewd, lascivious, and wanton people."

Move from the 1600s to the 1990s, and another "medical researcher," Richard Edwards, conducts an Internet survey of penis size. He logs the responses of more than three thousand men. Black penises were "slightly longer than whites ones in the flaccid state -- 3.7 inches for his black respondents, 3.4 for whites," Friedman writes. "The white erections were slightly longer than the black ones: 6.5 inches to 6.1." Friedman writes that researchers tell us to shorten most so-called "self measurements," given that peer pressure sneaks up on a cat, even when he's sending an email.

According to *The Penis Book* by Joseph Cohen: "The average length of a flaccid penis is 3.7 inches, with a diameter of 1.25 inches. The average length of an erect penis is 5.1 inches, with a diameter of 1.6 inches. Penises usually reach their manly max by the time a male turns 17. The shorter a guy's penis, the bigger it blossoms. Many chaps whose members are in the three-inch range when flaccid can look forward to organs that double in size when fully erect. Their hunkier buddies, on the other hand, almost never experience such growth ... although they're still ahead of the game."

When I'm in the pocket, I really don't need surveys or science to know that I shouldn't lose no sleep whatsoever over whether or not my best friends are packing. But given the funky uses of science when it comes to my Johnson, it don't hurt none to see the statisticians giving us little cats some love. Which frees me up to worry about the insomnia that's really wearing me out: Why my little Johnson ain't spending more time sliding up to its hilt inside some welcoming woman's body. Believe that! Especially, since it's connected to a halfway decent grown man, who is disease-free, drug-free, sane, and financially and emotionally solvent.

But I know I got to squash that whining, right now, and forevermore, cause at least I'm alive and functional and at peace with my humanity. Nowadays, unlike my historical Brothers of the Foreskin, I got analytical allies using their research to strengthen and reconfirm my inalienable membership in the human race. They remind me that when it comes to the Mythological Johnson, "...it's not really flesh-and-blood penises that shape a young man's perception that his penis is less than it is or should be," writes Susan Bordo, in *The Male Body*, "but a majestic imaginary member, against which no man's penis can ever measure up...."

And that majesty has been used against nobody more than me and my Johnson. I can hear the sad, bitter, knowing laughter of all the brothers who have been the object of the most irrational and hysterical game of the dozens ever devised. Locked down. Castrated. Dehumanized.

So get this:

When I hold my Johnson, I'm holding theirs.

Fondling like my life depends on it!

We ain't thinking about sex either!

I got our real Johnson on my mind, and my mind on our real Johnson. The one that's so real that all Black men got one.

Now run tell that!

Johnson Chronicles

Hair (Wet Dreams)

You'd think I could remember the exact date when the first strand of hair grew around my Johnson. I mean, when it happens, it's shocking to go from the bare skin of being a little boy to the downy beginnings that say you are on the way to becoming a grown man. I do know my pubic hair came with new stirrings between my legs, a new breathlessness in the presence of girls, and a new boldness that my father called "smelling my piss." I know that first strand gave me confidence that culminated at 16 with me growing my first 'fro and refusing Pops's demand that I let the neighborhood barber, Mr. Jackson, cut it into daddy's favorite crew-cut style.

Even TV commercials for Calgon bath oil fired me up. I'm up there trying to peek into the televised cleavage of the woman taking a bath in Calgon-scented water. Oh, the new pubic hair was strangling a brother's common sense! Still, I cannot stop time with sparkling 20-20. I cannot pinpoint that auspicious biological moment when Testosterone snapped open his eyes, yawned, checked his DNA clock, and started ordering hair to begin its itchy inching out the pores around my Johnson. Actually, the incoming hair was the signal of the Testing Time that I most welcomed. I proudly owned up to that evidence of Brother Testy's explosive, chemical wake-up-everybody!

But waking up to wet dreams!? Big nighttime convulsions that left my Fruit of the Looms wet with a silky circle? I was not feeling this demonstration of my body's turn. No way I was embracing a moment that felt too damn close to wetting the bed! And it seemed to happen when night was at its darkest. Even though I lived with two big brothers and my father (not to mention my mother, a pretty candid woman in her own right), I never ever thought about asking them why my penis was ambushing me in the middle of the night. I couldn't conceive that Pops, or my brothers, had themselves also once opened their eyes with a start and stared into the quiet darkness of a home asleep. I never imagined that they too had eased fearfully from under their blankets, tiptoed into the bathroom, and turned on the light to see a silver dollar of coagulating wetness staining their underwear. They, too, would have pulled away the waistbands to their Fruit of the Looms, looked down, only to see Johnson resting in contentment against that glistening circle.

When I stood alone in the bathroom, I never felt so in over my head. Here I got hair sprouting around a flexing dick that's spurting milk in the middle of the night, and ain't nobody alerted me to these new circumstances, and ain't nobody saying:

Shit, bro, it happened to me, too! It's normal, so just step out your drawers, use them to wipe away the wetness on your skin, and go on back to sleep.

Of course, in a perfect world, their counseling session would also come with advice on how I could slip my soiled underwear into the dirty clothes hamper the next day, without my parents noticing.

Truth be told, it wasn't like I had no idea about my body's upheavals. Thanks to books Moms had given me, I was up on the biological facts and figures. I knew about erections, night emissions, hair growth, my changing voice, that I was creating millions of sperm, and that my body was becoming fertile.

But man, those books couldn't begin to capture the visceral, electrifying sensations of puberty. Couldn't calculate the waves of pleasure throbbing within me, couldn't hint at the power that had me dancing like a white boy. Sex education books failed to help me understand the relentless confusion about my changes, my embarrassment, my inability to avoid tripping, and simply ask of those in the know:

What did y'all do when up jumped spring?

Now that my pubic hair is flecked with gray, I look back and wish for wet dreams. Wish my body was trembling

Johnson Chronicles

with such vitality that I got hard hearing the muffled scrape of my corduroy pants when I walked down the street. I wish that I could sit on the headboard of the twin bed I slept in as a teenager, and watch me squirm under the covers during Rapid Eye Movement, until my body stiffened during an adolescent orgasm. I would telepathically whisper into my own ear and say don't be afraid of waking your two brothers sleeping and snoring in the same room. They can't hear the explosion between your legs. They are probably holding their own Johnsons, as they dream about girl friends or fine-ass women they've seen during their daytime ramblings.

I'd whisper:

Breathe and lay still little brother. Feel the hot wetness cool off against your skin. Feel the stickiness without thinking it's yucky! Breathe and feel pleasure spiraling from your Johnson into your pelvis, into your chest, down your arms and legs, until your toes curl. Memorize this pulse and pledge your allegiance to it. Slide your hand down into your underwear and dip your finger into the moisture from which your son and your daughter will be formed. Be thankful that the sperm invisibly squirming – just like you, contorted in the dark of a D.C. night – do not contain mutations in their DNA that will cause your children to be malformed or miscarried or prone to Sudden Infant Death Syndrome or epilepsy or schizophrenia, autism or Sickle Cell Anemia.

I whisper:

Orgasms will make you laugh and boo hoo down on all fours. Orgasms will make you smile long past your desire to live with the mother of your son and daughter. Orgasms will compel you to leave the mother of your son and daughter. Orgasms will make you fuck women you don't even like. Orgasms will supercede love, intensify love, trump love.

The boy that I was hears the man that I am whisper encouragement and caution, advice and nonsense, all so we can learn to welcome without judgement, and with joy, the baby hair growing around our Johnson and the tablespoon of liquid ejaculated without control.

Pubic hair and wet dreams.

May sound like an early Prince song, but really they are the twin downbeats leading to hungry awareness of my Johnson. My scary beginnings, anxious beginnings, awkward beginnings. Before masturbation. Before sexual intercourse. Before the Blues of relationships with lovers.

Scary innocence when I needed my brothers to school me, but I was too naïve to ask, and they were too old to see through my naivete. Intimidating innocence, when I was too young, too full of cum, and too dumb to ask my father for his understanding, and he was too absorbed with work, paying bills, his Smirnoff-affirmed demons, his acceptance of crew-cuts and cryptic fatherhood roles, to fully initiate me through my body's awakening.

No harm, no foul, mind you. Cause within a couple of years I would be schooled about sexual citizenship by my oldest brother, even though I would still make hard-headed decisions against his teachings that would haunt me for a generation.

But on those damp nights I lay on my back, staring into the dark of a D.C. night, wondering how to tip-toe silently into the bathroom to change my underwear, I felt less like an unfolding man than like a trembling little boy. I felt my pubic hair growing long enough to let me know there was no turning back. I felt my pubic hair growing long enough to let me know a change gon come. I felt weak after coming without knowing why. I felt excited after coming without knowing why.

I no longer measure my changes by the clock.

I measure my changes by the pulsations of a body I've finally grown to know.

Johnson Chronicles

Truth. My Penis. Tall Tales

Johnson Chronicles

Truth and Tall Tales

You can't skate to graduate from the Round the Way Sexual Academy. Got to put in work. Hope your scars don't keloid and break mirrors when you ask who's the fairest of them all. Pray the damage you've done ain't the main ingredient of somebody's Blues.

I tried to skate. Had the gifts: mirror told me what I wanted to hear. Could open my mouth and have my own vagina monologues. Savored pussy like it was on a sushi menu. Told my boys everything they wanted to hear:

My Johnson so sweet ... I stir up her mother's first come.

My Johnson so sweet ... she sing My Favorite Things when I come.

My Johnson so big ...

And here let me hesitate another beat, cause I knew better, I've known better, but the need to talk trash sometimes overwhelmed *I've known rivers*. The need to flood the fictional record is so much a part of the brotherhood, even a dude with a modest joint, and a modest sex life, had to thicken the air with a tall tale:

My Johnson so big ... she got to ride me like Gladys Knight ride the Midnight Train to Georgia.

No doubt, my bravado should have been muted by the actual specs of my sex life, with its un-sensational ebb-and-flow. It should have been atrophied by inexperience, and weighted also by my awareness of how liquor or violence or power or inappropriate innuendo can shadow a childhood.

But revelations, illuminations, wisdom would come later. Knowing insights beyond punch lines lived on the horizon. I had years to live before I could tap into the courage to walk away when the lies started flying, or to check a brother (myself included) whose real life proved that he'd tripped trash talking into the fantastic. It would be years before I risked genuine disagreement based on principles, or dedicated myself to cultivating masculine safety, grace, integrity, and ethical commitment as keystones to a well-lived life.

No sir, not yet!

On that part of the journey, I was saturated by surging peer pressures. In fact, if truth be told, I was stunned by how genuinely joyful it felt to stand within the sheer theater of dudes testing bravado's limits. I was hypnotized by trash-talking one-liners so funny they made me laugh despite the outrageousness glowing around the edges of each word.

My Johnson so sweet she cancel Sunday dinner at her grandmama's house.

My Johnson so pretty she increase her tithe at church after we got naked the first time.

My Johnson so inspiring she subject to recite the Lord's Prayer when she push me on my back.

My Johnson might as well be called Savior much as she down on her knees.

Yes yes yes, with humble acknowledgment, I look back at when I was still a mouthpiece for my adolescent ventriloquist. Trilling with no rites of passage in sight. Unprepared to witness at the Scales of Doing the Right Thing. Opting for a vocabulary more suited to the Educated Fool, I buffed my amens to a sheen, and stripped them of all reverence. I strapped myself to a braggadocio with a bad case of emotional halitosis. Not to mention intellectual hocus-pocus.

So beneficial to me that my coat was eventually pulled by a gallery of HNICs. Big brothers. Pops & Them. Even peers hip to the salvation of vulnerability. They let me witness how they slowed their swagger to a stand still, inspired by reunion with a runaway daddy had a believable story on his breath, their mommy's heart attack while cradling first grandbaby, the gravity of a smell, a curve, a voice, a walk, even an intellect.

They sobered me up with looks of indigestion and vivacious recollections woven to help me stand with them at their crossroads, when intoxicating love or magisterial sex were the rewards that hung in the balance between bullshitting and taking it to the bridge. When they stood before lovers who wasn't having nothing to do with nobody who wasn't stripping their words of bullshit. They let me witness how they slowed their swagger to a stand still in order to imbue their halting testimony with simple honesty.

Finding only then:

Words flowing after steeping in the hot water of their boiling embarrassment, words believable after percolating in the pressure cooker of interpersonal originality, words only they could say out of mouths rejuvenated by long-breath, single meaning, and ethical signals that the one person who could sing in the face of life-changing challenge was describing the moment, in the moment, the best way he knew how.

And it worked. They tasted intoxicating love and magisterial sex. They were inspired to pass it on to youngsters they sensed and observed were tapping their capacity for quantum recalibration into a genuine maleness. They told me, yeah, revel in all the testosterone you can handle, but seek your deepest homeostasis by embracing all your manhood! Embrace the humanizing manhood of, let's say, a Deacon revered for his steady, unsung service to a small Southern church. Feel the humility, right, right, of a first-time father turned out after feeling his gestating child kick from within a mother's womb. Find the refreshment of becoming a grown-up, a grown man, who lives for the incandescence of tears let loose in the presence of un-orchestrated emotion.

Their voices echoed when I turned to my copy of *The Sacred Book for Haunted Lovers*. In the subsection, "Truth," I now found erudition grappling with itself in a quest for eloquence. I felt the tension of uncertainty, the galvanizing demands of a brother standing on the verge of getting it on. I was confronted by new questions. Spout

Truth. My Penis. Tall Tales

more tall tales? Or shape the sound of my own declarations of innocence before the Scales of Doing the Right Thing? Say anything to get over? Or become a man of my word? Cross my fingers behind my back during confession? Or utter oaths in the voice of a city boy grateful to the rural Virginia ancestry on Pops' side of the fam and his Moms' New York, New York pedigree?

I entered a new season with conviction. I could close my eyes tightly and feel myself evolving. I accepted the responsibilities of becoming an ethical man. In the face of a grown woman, I spoke my simple mind, instead of an R&B solo. I committed to passing lie-detector tests anywhere and everywhere, building my muscle, refusing to wait on my eulogy, or an aha moment within my twilight during last rites as I lay on my deathbed surrounded by loved ones.

The Sacred HNICs set me right! They were like Ghosts of Homeboys Past, who used their lives to teach me the lessons I'd need for my future. And as ethical guides, they never faked the funk. Offered no guarantees. Choose Truth over Tall Tales, not cause we say so, but because it feels right to you. You still bound to make mistakes. You still bound to get your ass caught in a vise. You still bound to be tested to your core.

And how I would need all their protection, all their recalibration, all their loving reminders, when my path intersected with that one nigger living like he ain't subject to no motherfucking ground rules. How their counsel cradled me, sustained me, steeled me, when the ugliest truth shredded every tall tale ever spoken in my life, after I learned that a man masquerading as my daughter's father had raped her, when she was 14. Violating her in secret for five years afterward. Violating his oaths to her mother and to his counseling profession, to his role as so-called stepfather. Fooling her mother. Fooling me. Fooling our extended family. Until my kid, then in her early 20s, found her public voice, and asked me to resist revenge and work with her to rebuild with her.

With the help of the legal system, we put the criminal fake father in jail, and through letters, time, counseling, courageous conversations, and love from another dimension, my child and I found a new stride that synchronized us deeply and inspired steady, mutual commitment to crafting a future of personal and public and joyful – but forever sober – testimony.

Truth and no tall tales!

Now I am guided by a humbling understanding that my Johnson Chronicles will forever rumble with the undertones of my confrontation with every expectation of Black manhood. Those undertones are the force come with coalescing, consolidating, into my richest definition of a man. I feel like, in my daily life, as I walk the sidewalks of my life, that I'm projecting a full-body MRI, colored with the clash of emotions that will forever test my constitution. I invisibly radiate gravitational waves that incorporate, yet go way beyond, anger, rage, vengeance, way beyond forgiveness, weakness, humility. My MRI body-double phases within and without, feels faint and almost overwhelmed by a brain flushed with negative emotions run amuck, with testicles inflamed and flooding me with testosterone-fueled images of my fists flying from an opaque body, my feet stomping his dark grimacing face. Imaginary actions, randomly violent, unsynchronized with my practical actions, constantly threaten my balance, as I make myself a way in this indifferent world.

Waves of terrible velocity push powerfully from a man who began throbbing into being when my kid said, *Dad, I don't want you to do nothing. I want you to have my back for the rest of my life.* And now, when I speak, out my mouth comes way more than just my own words. I speak in the amplified voices of all the friends and teachers who, soon as I open my mouth, instantaneously soothe or neutralize or fine-line all my simultaneous regrets that I didn't pimp-slap and choke his amoral ass, because I placed myself in service of the one true victim, my kid, my baby girl.

I had the chance, too.

... I was walking out the bathroom at the courthouse when he was coming in. How could this individual be going to take a piss without police escort? How could he even touch his own dick? His rape trial was about to start in a room just down the hall. Innocent until proven guilty my ass! Lightning at another crossroads and the flash showed me everything I had ever been taught about being a man:

I was supposed to have just killed Homeboy with my bare hands. Walked right up in his face, then pimp-slap him first, just to humiliate him, just to set the tone. Then I was supposed to choke him till his eyes rolled up in the back of his head. Until he foamed at the mouth. Shouted at his ass to confess, beg for mercy, atone. Stand over him when he dropped to his knees. Spit on him. Kick in his face. Stomp his nuts to bloody pulp. Overcome the guards running up to restrain me, grab a blackjack and jam it up his ass.

I could feel myself flickering, flaring up, solarizing. I inhaled sharply to halt my wilt and slide into incoherence. I gathered myself, decelerating into powerful homeostasis under the fluorescent lights of this courthouse corridor in Prince Georges County, Maryland. And slowly, steadily, I strengthened into a gentle, violet sound of my daughter's entreaty, like a gentle pin-prick, like a tender homing signal.

I saw the image of my daughter emanate from within me, slowly swirling outward in undulations of insight and compassion, circulating around me, her father, her daddy. The image did not project away from me toward this criminal, but instead softly congealed around me in a healing rhythm, as if dancing Tai Chi or playing Capoeira. Her powerful, pulsating image powerfully protected me from myself. She acknowledged my painful understandings, my scary surrender to hope, but she

Johnson Chronicles

suffused me, a Guardian Angel with 50 percent of my DNA, so I could maintain alignment with what she had to face, so I could find the stamina to respect the burden that only she carries. Standing within striking distance of this man, I swayed between the wind-shear of round the way masculinity and what my daughter implored of me. I also felt braced by the compassion of my brother-friends, who had all told me how proud they were that I was standing with my kid. And neither my friends nor my daughter asked me to fake how deeply wounded I was in my own way, as a father, but they reminded me to quietly expand my spiritual lungs, and find a soothing balance in my inner-ear. My daughter and my brothers illuminated me from within and kept it very simple for me.

She was the victim, not me. Her body was violated, not my rep. Her stepfather lied to her, macked her. I wasn't forced to lie in that bed. Watch him play with himself. My baby girl had the pages ripped out of her copy of *The Sacred Book for Haunted Lovers*! Walking toward the man whose Johnson Chronicles includes raping his step daughter, whose tall tales … how does a child molester boast…? – walking toward this miserable motherfucker is when I knew why vows are written in blood, why birth comes with pain, why I had a vasectomy.

Staring into his eyes (and did he just nod at me the way good brothers do when they love each other?), I kept my promise: walked back to the courtroom where my daughter was waiting for her daddy. There I didn't need a bible to make my oath. I swore my oath on the pages I stitched back into a new chapter of the Sacred Book:

Love means safety. Spreads an electrifying confidence through our bones until there ain't no doubt about who got your back. Truth got to trump tall tales! Even if he'd just hugged her for one second too long, cracked a sex joke in her presence, even if during talks about birds and the bees, his encouraging smile lingered or veered off into the slightest smirk, even if he casually remarked to her mother that she was becoming a beautiful young lady or glanced at her ass when she wore shorts and didn't see her as a kid – like I still do and she now over 30 years old! – then Love can't never come out the mouth ever again.

Love is safety. Love is sacrifice. Love is stamina for the right thing. Love is living through others. Facing up to our selfishness and then powering and begging or praying through that selfishness. Love is recognizing somebody else's rights. Love is, yeah, since we human, and biological, acknowledging that as a child enters puberty, she can become beautiful and sexy, and may even, in an unexpected, visceral moment, stir within a father, her Pops, a 'damn, that's my child?!' before his common sense and Home Training – his guides and gifts from loving HNICs and histories and customs – make him laugh, ground himself, so that he again becomes what loving fathers are: protectors, journey-agents, wisdom-keepers, even desperate prison guards struggling to hold off the inevitable blossoming of our daughters and sons.

I chose silence for her fake-father's broke-dick ass, but I pledged and knew that from then on, my daughter, my son, my lovers, would only hear out my mouth:

Nothing but simple, honest words ... shimmering ... original ... rejuvenated by long-breath, single meaning, and doing the right thing....

Cause I want to taste intoxicating love and magisterial sex. Revel in all the testosterone I can handle, and still simmer in a humanizing manhood, the refreshment of un-orchestrated emotion, the guarantee my touch, my Johnson, will always bring pleasure over pain.
I hear voices.

    Be grown or be gone!
    Take the journey.
    Squash the okie doke – the first step toward Enlightenment.
    What you stand for?

Johnson Chronicles

Who trusts you?
Can a child trust you?
Does Love trust you?
Answer ... answer from the place inside you, where no child stands in line for love ... then come out and play. Then your Johnson will be, like, a wick of incandescence not an emissary of ownership.

Declare yourself...to the All 'n All ...
Declare your Sins ... live your Atonement ...
Declare what's Right ...proclaim your Innocence...
Declare your Truth ... unleash your Reciprocity...
as a grown ass man:

I dangle before no child with my Johnson
I bogard no pussy with my Johnson
I enter no body unless I am invited
I spread no disease with my Johnson
I issue no false promises with my Johnson
I extort nobody with my Johnson
I castrate nobody with my Johnson
I deprive no one deserving of my Johnson
I snatch nobody's humanity with my Johnson
I muddy no water with my Johnson
I war on nobody with my Johnson
I lie on nobody with my Johnson
I gossip on nobody with my Johnson
I spread no rumors with my Johnson
I slander no other Johnson
I envy the pleasure of no other Johnson
I swear no oath against another Johnson
I perjure against no other Johnson
I turn no weaponry against another Johnson
I stare no other erect Johnson into impotence
I sour the pleasure of no other Johnson
I lose no friendship over my Johnson
I base no friendship on my Johnson
I build no house on my Johnson
I destroy no house with my Johnson

Truth. My Penis. Tall Tales

I revel in my flaccid Johnson
I exaggerate nothing about my erect Johnson
I atone for misunderstandings over my Johnson
I account for the hungers of my Johnson
I acknowledge any wrong done with my Johnson
I release all who wronged my Johnson
I hoard no pleasure unto my Johnson
I sacrifice to give pleasure with my Johnson
I show tenderness with my Johnson
I embrace wonder with my Johnson
I honor mystery with my Johnson
I sanctify love with my Johnson
I teach gratitude with my Johnson
I sow peace with my Johnson
I share serenity with my Johnson
I pray with my Johnson
I divine the All 'n All with my Johnson

What could these Declarations offer to the enlightenment of Homeboys in my wake?

What is Sin? Atonement? Right and Innocence, Truth and Reciprocity in the Lifetime Exercise of My Johnson?

The Big Black Dick ...
Truth?
Tall tale?
Johnson has become again a normal part of my body.

I feel Deepened. Reverent. Accomplished.

Johnson Chronicles

Truth. My Penis. Tall Tales

Johnson Chronicles

Up for the Down Stroke

Dudes swear we only need divine intervention to get our Johnsons up for the down stroke. When it comes to the basics, we never think of God. Got to pee? Just don't let it sting and we're cool. Let the poets and freak photographers drool that our Johnson is the dangling symbol of maleness. Let the ethical scientists theorize why our chromosomes voted for a penis to evolve from the multiplication ignited by Pops's sperm and Moms' ovum.

But stir up in the mix the potential for getting some sex? Let us need and want Homeboy to rise and represent? Let Mr. Johnson get temperamental? Oh, you better bet that then we will promise to go to Confession, or pray to the east, take yoga classes, or channel the ghost of Martin Luther King, Jr. whooping a Sunday sermon.

Cause deep down, we know how easy it is for soft to feel like a permanent condition:

Small penis during the Testing Time of adolescence. Early fatherhood and divorce. Custody battle. Guilt over leaving our kids' Moms. Money woes. Child support. Death of a 57-year-old mother way before her time.

Thank goodness I stopped eating meat in the 1970s.

Blessings on broccoli and tofu and fruit.

At least I'm doing my part for physiology, you know, for literally keeping the arteries open and the blood flowing. At least on the social science tip, to offset measurements of my American life at under 70 years, I don't smoke tobacco or weed, I don't drink hard liquor, and I don't dump Crisco-fried chicken and sausage and eggs into my diet everyday. I am dedicated to testing how long this fragile body of African descent can live, before I die and have to stand before the Scales of Doing the Right Thing.

Still, I sometimes wonder how I ever get hard.

I'm just happy to have a Johnson that works.

Truth. My Penis. Tall Tales

I have fallen through myth into love with my normal, natural penis. Resisting the historical signifying of theology and science and pornography, cause, typically, I don't exist whenever anybody get up on the soapbox.

There's only The Black Penis – capitalized, capped on, coveted.

There's no human being with a penis, there's always an "it," from the jungle, "our Mandingo," a monster cock too big to fit in the camera's frame, always pounding, banging, ripping, stabbing, jabbing, ramming, throbbing, always making some women's mouth water, or pussy submit, always causing her to heave and grimace and gasp or gush or gag.

Then I look at my Johnson.

He don't growl. He don't brag. Even when he grows – from excitement over a lover I wish for, a lover I'm hot for, shit, even I when I see some porn got the right big-dick brother with the right gasping woman – he's just my hard Johnson. Sensitive to caress, squeeze, kiss, lick, wetness, Mavis Staples moan, and, yes, some pounding and pelvic slapping that's bringing down the mutual holler of holiness, complete with grimaces of satisfaction and authority and deep penetration. Oh yeah, with the right lover, he is up for power sex, but, for real, he's just my Johnson. Healthy enough to cash in on chemistry. Grown enough to know he can't dip into every temptation. Subject to downtime now that I dig the difference.

He's just flesh and blood.

Ain't that a bitch, after all the danger and mystery, terror and magic, been invested in him. My Johnson, a Black Penis, is just flesh and blood. My dick is just flesh and blood. My Johnson cannot be manufactured in a maquiladora, cannot be stamped with a bar code, cannot be slandered or enjoyed without my permission. I know where he's been, when he's been there, whether he brought the noise, brought the funk. I know his weight in my hand and the gigahertz of his hungry pulsation.

Johnson Chronicles

He is the hippest penis on the planet, just so....

He's got the most nerve endings, but if I try a little tenderness, neutralize taboos with creativity and passion, trust and savor my hungers, my turn-ons, groove on my truth, my tall tales, I can transform my whole body into my Johnson.

With a perfect will to find his perfect fit, whenever prayer and position allow me to get up for the down stroke.

THE END

www.ingramcontent.com/pod-product-compliance
Lightning Source LLC
Chambersburg PA
CBHW032056150426
43194CB00006B/542